Threats to Civil Liberties:
RELIGION

John Allen

ReferencePoint Press®

San Diego, CA

About the Author

John Allen is a writer living in Oklahoma City, Oklahoma.

For more information, contact:
ReferencePoint Press, Inc.
PO Box 27779
San Diego, CA 92198
www.ReferencePointPress.com

Picture Credits:

Cover: 1001nights/iStockphoto.com
6: Monkey Business Images/Shutterstock.com
10: Drafting the Declaration of Independence (oil on canvas), Chappel, Alonzo (1828—87)/the Heckscher Museum of Art, Huntington, NY, USA/August Heckscher Collection/Bridgeman Images
13: Associated Press
19: Joseph Rey/AU/KRT/Newscom
23: GARO/Science Source
25: Ron Sachs/SIPA/Newscom
31: Associated Press
35: Erin Scott/Polaris/Newscom
36: Rick Wilking/Reuters/Newscom
42: iStockphoto.com
47: Alex Edelman/CNP/AdMedia/Newscom
53: Margaret Sanger, guilty of violating the state penal code by operating the first birth control clinic, 1917 (b/w photo)/Private Collection/Bridgeman Images
55: Joseph Sohm/Shutterstock.com
59: Hill Street Studios Blend Images/Newscom
62: Larry Strong/Contra Costa Times/Newscom
67: Associated Press

LIBRARY OF CONGRESS CATALOGING-IN-PUBLICATION DATA

Name: Allen, John, 1957– author.
Title: Threats to Civil Liberties: Religion / John Allen.
Description: San Diego: ReferencePoint Press, 2018. | Series: Threats to Civil Liberties | Includes bibliographical references and index.
Identifiers: LCCN 2018017502 (print) | LCCN 2018019448 (ebook) | ISBN 9781682824542 (eBook) | ISBN 9781682824535 (hardback)
Subjects: LCSH: United States—Religion—21st century. | Freedom of religion—United States—History—21st century. | Civil rights—United States—History—21st century.
Classification: LCC BL2525 (ebook) | LCC BL2525 .A348 2018 (print) | DDC 322/.10973—dc23
LC record available at https://lccn.loc.gov/2018017502

CONTENTS

Deep Divisions on Religious Freedom

On January 18, 2018, the Department of Health and Human Services (HHS) announced a new program it said was designed to promote religious liberty. The program offered protections for health care workers who refuse to treat patients on religious or moral grounds. The newly created Division of Conscience and Religious Freedom would support doctors, nurses, and other health care workers who object to performing abortions or referring women to abortion services because of their religious beliefs. In a ceremony for the announcement, Roger Severino, the HHS official who created the new division, stressed the importance of protecting religious liberty. According to Severino, "We are saying, with the launch of this division, you do not need to shed your religious identity, you do not need to shed your moral convictions to be a part of the public square."[1]

Not everyone saw the move in such a positive light. The new agency marked a sudden reversal of policy from previous years. Since 2012, the HHS had barred medical personnel from refusing to perform such services, seeking to protect patients from discrimination related to religious belief. Opponents of the new policy feared its effect on medical care. Larry T. Decker, the executive director of the Secular Coalition, said the policy would be "turning religious belief into yet another barrier between vulnerable patients and the health care they need. The right to conscience does not include the right to impose your conscience on others."[2]

A Debate That Goes Back to the Nation's Beginning

Controversy over the new HHS policy shows the deep divisions that exist among Americans over religious liberty and the proper role of religion in public life. Much of this friction is due to significant changes in social attitudes that began during the 1960s. Although the United States remains more religiously oriented than most other Western nations, the percentage of Americans who consider themselves religious has fallen in recent decades. According to a 2016 Gallup poll, a little more than 50 percent of Americans consider religion to be very important in their lives. This compares to 75 percent of people in 1952. Only around 36 percent of Americans regularly attend services at a church, synagogue, or mosque. Today 70 percent of Americans believe the influence of religion in US society is declining. Although there are more than three thousand religious groups in the nation, about 20 percent of Americans do not identify with an organized religion. Religious belief also relates to political opinions. Progressives and independents are much less likely to be strongly religious than conservatives. These differences have led to bitter debates about protections for religious belief—debates that go back to the founding of the nation.

> "We are saying, with the launch of this division, you do not need to shed your religious identity, you do not need to shed your moral convictions to be a part of the public square."[1]
>
> —Roger Severino, the director of the Office for Civil Rights at the HHS

The US Constitution guarantees religious liberty for all citizens. The First Amendment declares that "Congress shall make no law respecting an establishment of religion, or prohibiting the free exercise thereof."[3] The founders, who themselves belonged to different religious groups, sought to ensure there would be no national church like the Church of England. They wanted to keep church and state separate. They also were keenly aware that the Pilgrims, Puritans, and other early settlers came to North America so they could practice their chosen faith freely. The founders

A nurse discusses health care options with a patient. A new federal program protects health care workers who, because of their religious beliefs, refuse to discuss abortion services with patients or assist with these procedures.

aimed to prevent the government from penalizing citizens for their religious beliefs or practices. Thus, the Constitution affirmed freedom of worship as one of the bedrock principles of the new nation, along with freedom of speech and due process of law. And although the United States began as an overwhelmingly Christian nation—which it remains statistically to this day—the Constitution protects the right to follow any religion or no religion at all.

A Delicate Balance

Religious disputes in the United States rarely pit one faith against another. Instead, disagreements usually involve the proper role of government in relation to religious belief. In theory, the government maintains a stance of benevolent neutrality toward religion, neither promoting it nor discouraging it. In practice, however, balancing religious liberty with the rights of nonbelievers or those who oppose any government connection to religion can be difficult. For example, the Supreme Court has ruled that an event at a public school, such as a football game, must not begin with a prayer, which would be an unconstitutional support for religion. Yet the money people pay to see the game is printed with the words "In God We Trust." Life in the United States is filled with such ironies. "In America," says Irish psychologist and author Nigel Barber, "religion is much more a part of public life whatever the constitution says."[4]

The Supreme Court has also found that religious liberty can sometimes be outweighed by other government concerns, such as ending discrimination or defending free speech. In such cases, the government is said to have a compelling interest that tips the balance. Battles over this idea tend to be emotional. Whereas religious leaders often claim that the government is trampling on the rights of believers, their secular (or nonreligious) opponents fret that the government is giving in to superstition and unscientific claims. As Charles C. Haynes, the director of the Religious Freedom Center of the Newseum Institute in Washington, DC, notes, "When you have two important American principles coming into tension, into conflict with one another, our goal as Americans is to sit down and try to see if we can uphold both."[5]

"When you have two important American principles coming into tension, into conflict with one another, our goal as Americans is to sit down and try to see if we can uphold both."[5]

—Charles C. Haynes, director of the Religious Freedom Center of the Newseum Institute in Washington, DC

CHAPTER 1

The Wall of Separation

"Do you consider yourself an orthodox Catholic?"[6] The question from Senator Dick Durbin of Illinois was posed to Amy Barrett, a law professor at Notre Dame University who was nominated for a federal judgeship. Durbin, himself a Catholic, and his colleagues on the Judiciary Committee were holding hearings to determine Barrett's fitness for the bench. Several senators expressed concern that Barrett might let her strong religious views influence her decisions.

Public Duty Versus Private Belief

California senator Dianne Feinstein argued that Barrett's belief in Catholic dogma—the basic teachings of the Catholic Church—might conflict with her duty to rule on cases in an impartial manner. "Why is it that so many of us on this side have this very uncomfortable feeling that—you know, dogma and law are two different things," said Feinstein. "And I think in your case, professor, when you read your speeches, the conclusion one draws is that the dogma lives loudly within you, and that's of concern when you come to big issues that large numbers of people have fought for years in this country."[7]

Many opinion writers saw nothing wrong with Durbin's and Feinstein's comments. "The question of how [Barrett's] religious commitments will affect her decisions is fair game,"[8] wrote Boston College law professor Cathleen Kaveny in the *Washington Post*. The *New York Times* editorial page said the remarks were justified because the United States is a nation devoted to separation of church and state. Others, however, were troubled by the senators' line of questioning. A person's religious belief is a private matter, they said, with no relevance to performing a job. It certainly should not disqualify a candidate for the federal bench. Some pointed out that the US Constitution forbids any religious test for public office, and others quoted from a law journal article that Barrett had cowritten, declaring that judges must rely on the law, not the church's moral teaching, in deciding cases. Despite the controversy, in October 2017 the Senate voted to confirm Barrett for the Seventh Circuit Court of Appeals.

A Key Metaphor

The dispute over the Barrett hearings raises a fundamental issue about religious liberty in America: the idea that religious belief should remain separate from the workings of government. The First Amendment to the US Constitution set forth this principle in the so-called Establishment Clause, which forbids the establishment of religion by Congress. Thomas Jefferson, who wrote the Declaration of Independence and served as the third president of the United States, expressed the idea in a powerful metaphor that is still used today: the wall of separation.

Jefferson created the metaphor in response to a group of Baptists in Danbury, Connecticut, who had written to him complaining that their state's constitution did not protect minority churches like their own from interference by state lawmakers. In his reply, written on January 1, 1802, Jefferson aired his views on this subject. His letter shows his strong support for protecting religious liberty:

> Believing with you that religion is a matter which lies solely between Man & his God, that he owes account to none other for his faith or his worship, and that the legitimate powers of government reach actions only, & not opinions, I contemplate with sovereign reverence that act of the whole American people which declared that their legislature should

"make no law respecting an establishment of religion, or prohibiting the free exercise thereof," thus building a wall of separation between Church & State.[9]

Jefferson's metaphor has come to dominate the national conversation about religious freedom. It expressed in simple words his own interpretation of what the First Amendment means with regard to religion. It has become a key influence on law and policy covering religious rights. However, far from settling the question, the metaphor has also sparked debate about its meaning—and the original meaning of the First Amendment—for more than two centuries.

Jefferson's Views on Religious Liberty

Jefferson, like the other founders, held strong opinions on how the government should function. He also was a deeply religious

Thomas Jefferson (second from right) strongly believed that religious belief should remain separate from the workings of government. He and the other founders included this idea in the Declaration of Independence.

person. He believed that the order and beauty of the universe were proof of God's existence. At the same time, with his restless intellect, he rejected some of the basic teachings of the Christian church. He approved of the ideas of the Enlightenment in Europe, a movement that emphasized reason, tolerance, liberty, and education over superstition and bigotry. It also stressed the separation of church and state. Like other Enlightenment thinkers, Jefferson believed that one's faith—or absence of faith—is a private matter, so the government had no business meddling in questions of personal belief. As president he acted on this conviction, doing away with official days of fasting and thanksgiving, which to him seemed to favor the Christian religion.

Jefferson's political enemies often attacked him for what they saw as his un-Christian or even atheistic views. Their attacks only confirmed for him that disputes over religion did not belong in the halls of government or the public square. Jefferson believed such matters should be left to each person's conscience. Furthermore, he felt that the government's neutral position on religion would tend to promote tolerance for all faiths, which in turn would help produce a strong government and well-ordered society.

Jefferson had no illusions about human nature. He recognized the temptation to force others to bow to one's own beliefs. He also knew a free society must always be able to balance extremes. Jefferson himself thought the religious views of his fellow citizens were mostly misguided, but he still gave the idea of religious liberty his full support. "It does me no injury for my neighbor to say there are twenty gods or no god," he wrote in *Notes on the State of Virginia*. "It neither picks my pocket, nor breaks my leg."[10] Thus, Jefferson was as devoted to the Free Exercise Clause—the right to worship freely as one chooses— as to the Establishment Clause. It was Jefferson, after all, who had insisted that the Constitution must contain the Bill of Rights, clearly setting forth these ideas about religious freedom. His wall of separation was, in effect, raised at the nation's founding.

The Movement Toward Strict Separation

Jefferson's wall of separation metaphor became widely known as the separation of church and state. Contrary to popular belief, this phrase does not appear in the Constitution. It is constantly used as shorthand for the Establishment Clause in the First Amendment, which prohibits government from establishing an official religion. Some insist that the phrase is a useful guide for preventing religions from playing a formal role in government. Others argue that the phrase has been interpreted in ways that run counter to Jefferson's original meaning. Both sides of the political debate over religious freedom have expressed strong feelings about the phrase and how it has been used and abused.

The phrase *separation of church and state* did not appear in a Supreme Court decision until 1879, more than fifty years after Jefferson's death. In upholding a law against bigamy or plural marriage, the court noted that the phrase had become an authoritative reading of the First Amendment's reach and effect. The first Supreme Court case to use the Establishment Clause directly in a decision was *Everson v. Board of Education* in 1947. In *Everson*, the court extended restrictions on religion to state governments as well as the federal government. Justice Hugo Black referred to Jefferson's famous phrase as he described the scope of the restrictions:

> The "establishment of religion" clause of the First Amendment means at least this: Neither a state nor the Federal Government can set up a church. Neither can pass laws which aid one religion, aid all religions, or prefer one religion over another. . . . No tax in any amount, large or small, can be levied to support any religious activities or institutions, whatever they may be called, or whatever form they may adopt to teach or practice religion. . . . In the words of Jefferson, the clause against establishment of religion by law was intended to erect a "wall of separation between Church and State."[11]

Both secular liberals and religious conservatives accepted the separation of church and state as the basis of church-state legal decisions. Yet from the 1940s until the late 1980s, the Supreme Court's rulings in cases involving religious rights increasingly supported secularism. Words like *absolute* and *uncompromising* were used to describe the scope of the Establishment Clause. After *Everson*, the court interpreted the Establishment Clause as setting very strict limits on how government could interact with religion. This became known as strict separation. It led the court to end prayer and Bible reading in public schools, disallow government funding for religious schools, and remove displays of religious symbols from public property.

Experts including Erwin Chemerinsky, an attorney and law professor who argued a major Establishment Clause case in 2005, strongly approved of strict separation. Chemerinsky claimed that a stone slab displaying the Ten Commandments on the grounds

A stone slab depicting the Ten Commandments stands on the grounds of the Texas state capitol. A legal challenge seeking removal of the religious symbol from public property failed.

of the Texas state capitol was an unconstitutional support for religion. The court eventually allowed the Texas monument to remain in place, but it ruled against such displays inside two courthouses in Kentucky. In the court's view, the Texas monument was a valid tribute to the nation's religious and legal history, but the displays inside the Kentucky courthouses crossed the line into promoting religious ideas. "The reason that I agreed to handle the Ten Commandments case is that I believe deeply that our government should be secular," said Chemerinsky. "It should not be affiliated with any religion and it should not advance any religion. But I also know that those who are on the other side believe just as deeply that they want their government to be religious, not secular."[12]

> "[The federal government] should not be affiliated with any religion and it should not advance any religion."[12]
>
> —Erwin Chemerinsky, an attorney and law professor

A Misreading of Jefferson's Views

Chemerinsky was correct about his opponents' beliefs. Not surprisingly, what has pleased secular scholars has been hugely disappointing to those on the other side. As more rulings were guided by strict separation, many feared that religion was being eliminated from public life in America. Justice Black had written in *Everson* that the wall of separation "must be kept high and impregnable. We could not approve the slightest breach."[13] Religious believers felt as if they were being walled off from public life in America.

Those in favor of a religious influence on government argued against the idea of strict separation. They claimed that Jefferson's views on religion were being distorted to further the cause of secularism. Jefferson, they noted, was certainly not an atheist, as some of his enemies had charged during his lifetime. And they insisted that Jefferson would not have supported ideas of strict separation. For example, as president he approved the use of federal funds to build churches and spread the Christian faith among Native American tribes. Some scholars also pointed out that Jefferson's wall between church and state actually had more to do with federalism—the separation of federal and state powers—than with separation of church and state. Although Jefferson, as president, opposed setting up religious holidays at the federal level, as governor of Virginia he had proclaimed a day for "public and solemn thanksgiving and prayer to Almighty God."[14] He believed that, according to the Constitution, states could officially support religion in ways the federal government could not.

Experts such as Daniel Dreisbach, a law professor at American University, argue that the high wall of strict separation was not Jefferson's idea but Justice Hugo Black's. To Dreisbach, the version pushed by Black, and by secularists today, does not support religious liberty. Instead, he believes it tries to eliminate religious influence from government entirely, at the federal, state, and local levels. "All too often, the wall of separation is used to silence the church and to limit its reach into public life," Dreisbach declares, "but it is rarely used to restrain the civil state's meddling in, and restraint of, the church."[15] In arguments for *Van Orden v. Perry*, the Texas Ten Commandments case, Justice Anthony Kennedy echoed the thoughts of many religious conservatives in America who feared that faith was no longer welcome in public life. "There is this obsessive concern over any mention of religion," said Kennedy, "[and] that shows a hostility toward religion."[16]

> "All too often, the wall of separation is used to silence the church and to limit its reach into public life, but it is rarely used to restrain the civil state's meddling in, and restraint of, the church."[15]
>
> —Daniel Dreisbach, a law professor at American University

Three Ways of Looking at the Establishment Clause

For decades the idea of strict separation has generally held sway in America. Organizations, including the American Civil Liberties

Union (ACLU) and Americans United for Separation of Church and State, have worked to defend their vision of Jefferson's wall of separation. They believe the government should remain completely secular. To them, the proper place for religion is in the home, the church, the mosque, or the synagogue. They seek to protect the rights of nonbelievers, religious minorities, and those of different sexual identities. They are always alert to undue religious influence among judges, lawmakers, educators, and government officials.

Yet strict separation is only one of three main views of the Establishment Clause among legal scholars. A second version

The Wall of Separation Should Be Absolute

Critics of Democratic presidential candidate John F. Kennedy claimed his Catholic faith would influence his decisions as president. In a speech on September 12, 1960, Kennedy affirmed his belief in the wall of separation:

> I believe in an America where the separation of church and state is absolute—where no Catholic prelate would tell the President (should he be Catholic) how to act and no Protestant minister would tell his parishioners for whom to vote—where no church or church school is granted any public funds or political preference—and where no man is denied public office merely because his religion differs from the President who might appoint him or the people who might elect him.

> I believe in an America that is officially neither Catholic, Protestant, nor Jewish . . . where no religious body seeks to impose its will directly or indirectly upon the general populace or the public acts of its officials.

NPR, "Transcript: JFK's Speech on His Religion," December 5, 2007. www.npr.org.

The Wall of Separation Should Not Be Absolute

During the 2012 presidential campaign, Republican candidate Rick Santorum took issue with Kennedy's speech on the wall of separation. In a television interview, Santorum said,

> I don't believe in an America where the separation of church and state is absolute. The idea that the church can have no influence or no involvement in the operation of the state is absolutely antithetical [opposed] to the objectives and vision of our country. . . .
>
> This is the First Amendment. The First Amendment says the free exercise of religion. That means bringing everybody, people of faith and no faith, into the public square. Kennedy for the first time articulated the vision saying, no, faith is not allowed in the public square. . . . It was an absolutist doctrine that was abhorrent [terrible] at the time of 1960. And I went down to Houston, Texas 50 years almost to the day, and gave a speech and talked about how important it is for everybody to feel welcome in the public square. People of faith, people of no faith, and be able to bring their ideas, to bring passions into the public square and have it out.

ABC News, "'This Week' Transcript: GOP Candidate Rick Santorum," February 26, 2012. www.abcnews.go.com.

holds that under the Establishment Clause the government must remain neutral toward religion. It should not favor religion over secularism, or secularism over religion. No religion, whether Christianity, Islam, Judaism, or Buddhism, should be treated differently from any other. Justice Sandra Day O'Connor was one of the most prominent legal minds to hold this view. She thought remaining neutral in this way meant the government should never endorse any particular religion, or religion in general, through symbols, words, or actions. Those like Justice O'Connor, who favor this neutral-government approach, view religious belief as a vital part of American history. They want religion to remain, in all its diversity, an important part of society.

A third view interprets the Establishment Clause quite differently from the other two. This view sees the United States as a religious nation founded on the belief in God. The government may interact with religion in any number of ways as long as it does not set up a national church or coerce membership in any religion. This approach is often called accommodationist because it seeks to accommodate, or offer protection for, religious believers in relation to the government. Religious conservatives tend to support this view of the Establishment Clause because it secures for religion a much larger role in public life. Mark David Hall, a political science professor at George Fox University, says that America has made accommodations for people of faith throughout its history. As Hall notes, "America's laudable history of protecting religious citizens from otherwise valid laws makes it clear not only that it is possible to protect 'the sacred rights of conscience' and promote the common good, but also that religious accommodations *themselves* promote the common good."[17]

In 1993 Congress advanced the accommodationists' cause by passing the Religious Freedom Restoration Act (RFRA), which expanded existing law. The law states that "Government shall not substantially burden a person's exercise of religion even if the burden results from a rule of general applicability."[18] This means that a person can be exempted from a law meant to apply to all citizens if that law interferes with the person's right to religious belief. For example, Quakers, who object to killing under any circumstances, were exempt from military draft laws from the time of the Civil War through the Vietnam War. President Bill Clinton, who signed the RFRA, said it subjects the federal government to "a very high level of proof before it interferes with someone's free exercise of religion."[19] Those devoted to strict separation felt outraged. They began to worry that Jefferson's wall was in danger.

Members of the Quaker faith take part in a worship service. Quakers object to killing under any circumstances and therefore have been exempt from military drafts during wartime.

Breaching the Wall of Separation

Today there are signs that religious accommodation is indeed punching holes in the wall of separation. Although divided on religious issues, the Supreme Court seems more willing to grant exceptions to strict separation of church and state. This has raised concerns among liberal secularists that right-wing conservatives are using religious liberty to erode laws and policies they do not like. According to opinion writer Catherine Rampell, "Times have changed. Now the mantra is: If you can't beat 'em, out-God 'em. Don't like same-sex marriage, contraception, HIV testing or even child labor laws? Never you worry: Just say that a higher power has exempted you, even if your exemption means trampling on other people's rights."[20]

> "Don't like same-sex marriage, contraception, HIV testing or even child labor laws? Never you worry: Just say that a higher power has exempted you, even if your exemption means trampling on other people's rights."[20]
>
> —Political journalist Catherine Rampell

Despite all the strong feelings about accommodation, sometimes it leads to practical outcomes both sides can live with. In *Trinity Lutheran Church of Columbus v. Comey* (2017), the Supreme Court ruled 7–2 that states cannot exclude a church from a state-run program simply because of the church's religious identity. This allowed Trinity Lutheran to participate in a Missouri program that resurfaced playgrounds with shredded tires for children's safety. Yet this support for the Free Exercise Clause over strict separation promised larger battles to come. Jefferson's wall of separation, one of the key elements of American democracy, almost certainly will face serious challenges in the years ahead.

CHAPTER 2

Protecting Women's Health

On June 30, 2014, angry voices filled the air on the National Mall in Washington, DC. Signs waved by a crowd of protesters outside the Supreme Court expressed bitter disagreement about the legal issue at stake. The sentiments included "Bosses—Keep Your Business in the Boardrooms Not Our Bedroom" and "Pro-Life Is Pro-Woman." The court was due to hand down its decision in *Burwell v. Hobby Lobby*, a case that pitted women's reproductive rights against religious rights under the Free Exercise Clause.

Objections to Coverage for Birth Control

Health care issues in the United States often intersect—some would say collide—with questions of religious liberty. The *Hobby Lobby* case, one of the most controversial in recent years, addressed health insurance coverage for contraception, or birth control. The 2010 Affordable Care Act (ACA), often called Obamacare, was designed to provide low-cost health care plans for Americans who otherwise lacked insurance coverage. In addition, the ACA set strict standards for what private health care plans must cover. It required employers to cover the cost for birth control pills and other methods of contraception for their female employees. Among these birth control options were four types, including the so-called morning-after pill and intrauterine devices (IUDs), which some consider to be forms of abortion. Many medical experts dispute this claim, which is based on the idea that human life begins at conception, but the government did not pursue this point in its defense.

The Greens, a family of evangelical Christians who owns the multibillion-dollar arts and crafts chain Hobby Lobby, objected to the government mandate that they include morning-after pills and IUDs in their insurance coverage. The Greens did not object to the other forms of birth control in the mandate and said they did not want to make health care decisions for their employees. But they contended that paying for abortion drugs or devices for female employees violated their constitutional rights to free exercise of religion. If they lost the case, their failure to comply with the law promised to be expensive: it meant a fine of $100 a day for each employee affected.

Opponents claimed the issue was not religious freedom but simple economics. They argued that companies like Hobby Lobby and Conestoga Wood Specialties, a Pennsylvania firm involved in a similar case, were putting the health of lower-income women at risk. Many would have to make difficult choices on which birth control method to use based on financial means. IUDs, which are very effective methods of birth control, can cost $1,000 each. Obamacare supporters pointed to research findings that one-third of eligible women would change their birth control method if cost were no issue. "Women already have an income gap," said Marcia Greenberger, copresident of the National Women's Law Center. "If these companies prevail, they'll have a health insurance gap, too."[21]

Also at issue was the ability of family-owned companies like Hobby Lobby to make decisions free from government interference. Legal experts felt that Hobby Lobby and Conestoga were swimming against a powerful tide by challenging the health care mandate. According to a study by the Kaiser Family Foundation, more than 85 percent of large US employers had already offered their employees complete birth control coverage even before the ACA was passed. There were very few objections to the mandate among public corporations.

A Narrow Decision

The Supreme Court's majority drew upon the RFRA in ruling 5–4 in favor of Hobby Lobby. In his lead opinion, Justice Samuel Alito

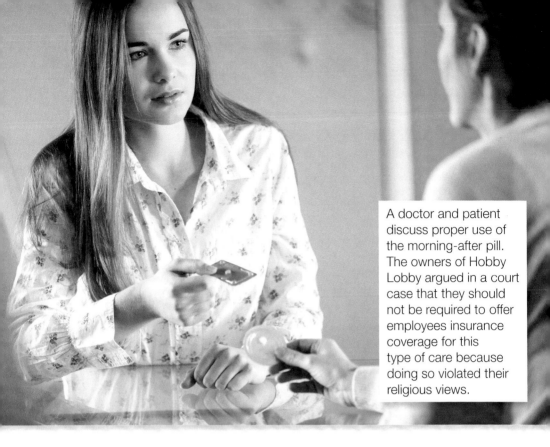

A doctor and patient discuss proper use of the morning-after pill. The owners of Hobby Lobby argued in a court case that they should not be required to offer employees insurance coverage for this type of care because doing so violated their religious views.

noted that the RFRA required the government to use other means to accomplish a regulatory purpose if a law interfered with someone's free exercise of religion, and there were alternative options available. The government had already allowed nonprofit companies to opt out of insurance coverage for contraceptives on religious grounds. In such cases, the insurers themselves paid for employees' birth control. It was a small step, the court's majority decided, to do the same for Hobby Lobby and other for-profit companies. As Alito explained,

> The plain terms of RFRA make it perfectly clear that Congress did not discriminate . . . against men and women who wish to run their businesses as for-profit corporations in the manner required by their religious beliefs. Our responsibility is to enforce RFRA as written, and under the standard that RFRA prescribes, the [ACA] contraceptive mandate is unlawful.[22]

However, Alito also insisted the ruling was not a license to discriminate:

> This decision concerns only the contraceptive mandate and should not be understood to hold that all insurance-coverage mandates, e.g., for vaccinations or blood transfusions, must necessarily fall if they conflict with an employer's religious beliefs. Nor does it provide a shield for employers who might cloak illegal discrimination as a religious practice.[23]

"This decision concerns only the contraceptive mandate and should not be understood to hold that all insurance-coverage mandates . . . must necessarily fall if they conflict with an employer's religious beliefs."[23]

—Justice Samuel Alito in *Burwell v. Hobby Lobby*

Hobby Lobby's owners saw the ruling as a triumph for First Amendment rights. "Our family is overjoyed by the Supreme Court's decision," said Barbara Green, one of the company's cofounders. "The Court's decision is a victory, not just for our family business, but for all who seek to live out their faith."[24] Many conservatives thought the decision was a long overdue rebuke to liberal health care policies. "Hey liberals, guess what?!" tweeted Atlanta radio host Erick Erickson. "Your birth control isn't your boss's business now! Thanks Supreme Court!"[25]

Landmark—or Minefield?

The *Hobby Lobby* case may prove to be a landmark in First Amendment law—or a potential minefield, as its opponents claim. Legal scholars expect the decision to influence religious liberty issues for years to come. Some pointed out that the ruling was not as sweeping as it could have been. The court limited its focus to the RFRA promise that laws must not pose an undue burden on people's religious beliefs. As Alito observed, for Hobby Lobby's owners to follow their religious conscience would have cost them a fine of up to $1.3 million per day, or about $475 million a year. "If these consequences do not amount to a substantial burden, it is hard to see what would,"[26] he wrote.

Nonetheless, many expressed fears for the future of strict separation. Critics foresaw a flood of religious objections to all sorts of laws and regulations. Such an outcome, they said, could place the rights of vulnerable minorities at risk, not to mention their health. "Justice Alito goes out of his way to say that this decision is limited to just this case," said Louise Melling, the deputy legal director of the ACLU. "Somehow the question of contraception is different from other forms of discrimination. Somehow the question of contraception is different from other forms of health care. We've all seen that playbook before."[27]

Three of the no votes were cast by the women on the court. Justice Ruth Bader Ginsburg strongly disagreed with the decision, believing it could affect compliance with workplace laws across the nation. In her thirty-five-page dissenting opinion, Ginsburg wrote,

US Supreme Court justice Ruth Bader Ginsburg (pictured) strongly disagreed with the Court's decision in the *Hobby Lobby* case. She argued that the decision could lead to widespread violations of workplace laws.

"[The ruling] discounts the disadvantages religion-based opt-outs impose on others—in particular, employees who do not share their employer's religious beliefs." For Ginsburg, it was plain that the court had opened itself to all sorts of legal objections on religious grounds. Her opinion ended with a warning: "The Court, I fear, has ventured into a minefield."[28]

Many legal scholars agreed. Among them are three prominent law professors—Micah Schwartzman, Richard Schragger, and Nelson Tebbe—who predicted the *Hobby Lobby* decision would have far-reaching negative effects. They compared it to the *Citizens United* case, which recognized free speech rights for corporations as if they were individuals. After the *Hobby Lobby* case, they noted, for-profit businesses would now be treated like churches and non-profit religious groups. "For the first time," said the professors,

> the court has interpreted a federal statute, the Religious Freedom Restoration Act (or RFRA), as affording more protection for religion than has ever been provided under the First Amendment. . . . The court has eviscerated [gutted] decades of case law and, having done that, invites a new generation of challenges to federal laws, including those designed to protect civil rights.[29]

Ruling Against the Little Sisters of the Poor

As a multibillion-dollar business, Hobby Lobby may not have been the most sympathetic defender of religious rights. That was not the case with another recent high-profile plaintiff: a group of Catholic nuns called the Little Sisters of the Poor. Founded in 1839, the Little Sisters are a religious order with about twenty-three hundred members in the United States. They are dedicated to helping the poor and elderly. Like Hobby Lobby and Conestoga Wood Specialties, the Little Sisters objected to the ACA's requirement to provide birth control as part of women's health insurance coverage. As political writer Emma Green noted,

> When the Little Sisters of the Poor filed a complaint against the Affordable Care Act's contraceptive mandate in 2013, they joined a host of other religious charities and colleges that claimed the law placed a burden on their free exercise of their religion. But the sisters stood out: If nuns claim a law violates their conscience, who's to tell them they're wrong?[30]

The Little Sisters' name and history of good works led many in the media to report on their case in a sympathetic light. However, some asked why these women, who are mostly elderly themselves and have taken a vow of celibacy, were suing the government over birth control? The answer lay in religious belief and conscience. Few could doubt the sincerity of women who had dedicated their lives to their beliefs. In explaining the Little Sisters' determination to pursue the case, Sister Constance Carolyn said, "We vow to devote our lives specifically to the service of the elderly poor, but the unborn are no less worthy of reverence and protection than the frail seniors we serve every day."[31]

"If nuns claim a law violates their conscience, who's to tell them they're wrong?"[30]

—Political writer Emma Green

On July 14, 2015, the Tenth Circuit Court of Appeals ruled against the Little Sisters. The court explained that after the *Hobby Lobby* case, the federal government had made substantial efforts to accommodate nonprofit groups that objected to birth control coverage on religious grounds. An organization like the Little Sisters could simply sign a two-page form stating their objection to the mandate. This would authorize the government to make sure that a third party, whether the group's insurance company or a government agency, would pay for birth control coverage. The

A Company Should Not Have to Provide Its Employees Birth Control Coverage

In *Burwell v. Hobby Lobby* (2014), the Supreme Court ruled that a for-profit company like Hobby Lobby could not be forced to provide its employees with birth control methods to which it objected on religious grounds. Justice Samuel Alito wrote for the majority,

> RFRA's question is whether the mandate imposes a substantial burden on the objecting parties' ability to conduct business in accordance with their religious beliefs. The belief of the . . . Greens implicates [raises] a difficult and important question of religion and moral philosophy, namely, the circumstances under which it is immoral for a person to perform an act that is innocent in itself but that has the effect of enabling or facilitating the commission of an immoral act by another. It is not for the Court to say that the religious beliefs of the plaintiffs are mistaken or unreasonable.

Quoted in Justia, "Burwell v. Hobby Lobby Stores, Inc., 573 U.S. ___ (2014)." https://supreme.justia.com.

court decided that signing the form was not a significant burden on the group and thus did not violate the RFRA.

A Major Victory for the Little Sisters

Yet the Little Sisters still found the circuit court's decision unacceptable. To them, signing a waiver form was indeed a significant burden. It amounted to condoning abortion. The Little Sisters appealed the case to the Supreme Court, which bundled it with several other similar cases brought by nonprofit religious groups.

Court observers predicted a 4–4 tie that would allow the lower court's decision to stand. (The court temporarily had only eight justices instead of the usual nine.) Yet on May 16, 2016,

A Company Should Have to Provide Its Employees Birth Control Coverage

In a scathing thirty-five-page dissent, Justice Ruth Bader Ginsburg declared that Hobby Lobby's employees should not be deprived of birth control coverage simply because of the owners' religious beliefs:

> The statutory scheme of employer-based comprehensive health coverage involved in these cases is surely binding on others engaged in the same trade or business as the corporate challengers here, Hobby Lobby and Conestoga. . . . No doubt the [owners] and all who share their beliefs may decline to acquire for themselves the contraceptives in question. But that choice may not be imposed on employees who hold other beliefs. Working for Hobby Lobby or Conestoga, in other words, should not deprive employees of the preventive care available to workers at the shop next door.

Quoted in Justia, "Burwell v. Hobby Lobby Stores, Inc., 573 U.S. ___ (2014)," https://supreme.justia.com.

the court surprised almost everyone by handing down a unanimous decision. It vacated, or wiped away, all the lower court's rulings in the bundled cases. The justices ordered the lower court to find a way to provide birth control coverage without any collaboration by the Little Sisters and the other nonprofits. In other words, the court ruled that even having to sign a paper objecting to birth control coverage was a substantial burden for the Little Sisters and other plaintiffs. Although the issue was not settled, the decision handed the Little Sisters a major victory over the government.

Opponents worried that the court was abandoning women's health to accommodate religious belief in every way. And some, like Stephanie Mencimer of the progressive magazine *Mother*

Jones, pointed out that the Little Sisters case still involved crucial health care issues for women:

> As much as their chastity was supposed to embarrass the Obama administration for trying to force nuns to provide contraceptive coverage, it turns out that sometimes even nuns need birth control. After all, birth control pills are prescribed for a wide variety of health problems, such as irregular menstrual bleeding, that have nothing to do with preventing pregnancy—and many of these health problems are widespread among older women, including nuns.[32]

In November 2017, the Little Sisters received more positive news, this time from President Donald Trump. To fulfill a campaign promise, Trump announced that religious nonprofits like the Little Sisters would be exempted from the ACA's birth control mandate entirely. One month later the states of California and Pennsylvania sued the federal government to challenge the new rule. Each state's attorney general claimed it illegally limited women's access to contraceptives. Few observers will be surprised if the case once again winds up at the Supreme Court.

Requirements for Antiabortion Centers

Forty-five years after *Roe v. Wade* made abortion legal in the United States, the issue continues to inflame passions among women's rights activists and defenders of religious liberty. The latest controversy deals with a California law passed in 2015. The law requires licensed pregnancy counseling centers to display information about California's free or low-cost programs for birth control and abortion services. Religious-oriented centers, some of which are run by churches, object to posting the notices. Managers claim the requirement violates their free speech rights. They argue that the whole point of their facilities, called

The Little Sisters of the Poor (speaking to the media in 2015) objected to the Affordable Care Act requirement that health insurance for female employees include birth control coverage. They contended that the law placed a burden on the free exercise of religion.

crisis pregnancy centers, is to steer women away from abortion. Instead, they are being forced to deliver a message that goes against their beliefs—to act "as a ventriloquist's dummy for a government message,"[33] according to Jay Sekulow of the American Center for Law and Justice.

Although abortion is not at issue in the case, advocates for women's health fear a slippery slope in which religious objections censor practical messages about health care options. California's attorney general, Xavier Becerra, says the law provides women with vital information. According to Becerra, more than half of the state's seven hundred thousand pregnancies each year are unplanned. Many women are unaware of California's subsidized programs to help them. The organization NARAL Pro-Choice California reports that 41 percent of California counties have no abortion provider, but 91 percent have at least one religious-based crisis pregnancy center. Impoverished young women in rural towns often have trouble getting to a counseling center where birth control and abortion are discussed as options.

For example, in California's Central Valley town of Visalia, young women like twenty-one-year-old Rosalinda Hernandez-Guzman must travel long distances to reach an abortion provider. When Hernandez-Guzman became pregnant, she considered getting an abortion for financial reasons. She and her farmworker husband already had an infant, and they lacked money to rent a car or take public transportation to a full-service clinic in a large city. In such cases, a nearby crisis pregnancy center often seems to be the best solution. But these centers urge clients to forego abortion in favor of other options, so clients like Hernandez-Guzman may not be informed about all the free services California provides.

Heated Battles Ahead

With these facts in mind, many legal experts think the California law is not only helpful but perfectly fair. As Erwin Chemerinsky notes,

> The law does nothing other than require this information be posted on a wall for patients to see. No one is required to say anything. Nor is there any requirement for providing contraception information or abortion referrals. The law is just to make sure that women know the services that the State of California makes available and whether the facility is unlicensed.[34]

Chemerinsky also claims that religious-based crisis pregnancy centers sometimes offer false medical information. He says some employ scare tactics to steer clients away from seeking abortions. Nonetheless, in the current climate of the RFRA, many legal scholars doubt the Supreme Court will uphold the California law.

When it comes to issues of women's health, religious liberty and government priorities repeatedly clash. For now, the RFRA and related Supreme Court decisions seem to have tipped the scales toward the free exercise of religion. Certainly, there will be heated battles ahead as women's rights activists pursue their own vision for health care in America.

CHAPTER 3

Same-Sex Marriage and Religious Objections

In politically divided times, even a trip to the bakery can trigger a constitutional issue. In July 2012 Charlie Craig and David Mullins walked into Masterpiece Cakeshop in Lakewood, Colorado, to order a custom-made cake for their upcoming wedding reception. Jack Phillips, the owner of the shop, refused the couple's request. He explained that he opposed same-sex marriage due to his Christian beliefs and did not want to do anything that would seem to endorse same-sex weddings. Craig and Mullins responded by filing charges of discrimination against Phillips. It is against the law in Colorado to discriminate on the basis of sexual orientation. This applies to public businesses such as restaurants and hotels—and bakeries.

The case wound its way through Colorado courts and administrative agencies for years. The Colorado Civil Rights Commission, a state judge of administrative law, and the Colorado Court of Appeals all ruled in the couple's favor. By the time Phillips appealed the case to the Supreme Court, the whole nation knew about the Colorado cake shop incident. Observers stressed that the stakes were high. "If the Supreme Court rules in favor of Masterpiece Cakeshop, it could open a loophole in federal and state civil rights laws that lets people like Phillips get around bans on discrimination by citing their rights to free speech and religious expression," legal reporter German Lopez wrote in 2017. "That could lead to more—and totally legal—discrimination, not just from Phillips or bakers but from all businesses that serve the public."[35]

A Movement Toward Tolerance

American society has undergone rapid change on the issue of gay marriage since the incident that sparked *Masterpiece Cakeshop v. Colorado Civil Rights Commission*. According to the Pew Research Center, 62 percent of Americans now support same-sex marriage. When Craig and Mullins requested their wedding cake in 2012, less than half of Americans supported it, and only a few states recognized same-sex unions. Twenty-five states had specifically banned gay marriage since the passage of the 1996 Defense of Marriage Act, which defined marriage as being solely between a man and a woman. But in the last decade, attitudes toward same-sex marriage became more positive. Although many conservative religious believers remained opposed, a majority of Americans came to accept it. Politicians and pundits who had tiptoed around the issue increasingly came out in support of gay marriage. Like other states, Colorado acted in response to these changes. It began issuing marriage licenses to same-sex couples in 2014. (Craig and Mullins had actually gotten married in Massachusetts and were planning a reception for friends in Colorado.)

The following year, in *Obergefell v. Hodges*, the Supreme Court made same-sex marriage legal everywhere in America, meaning marriages must be performed and recognized in all the states the same as for opposite-sex couples. The court ruled that the fundamental right to marry is guaranteed to same-sex couples by the Due Process Clause and the Equal Protection Clause of the Fourteenth Amendment. Professor William Baude of the University of Chicago Law School saw the *Masterpiece Cakeshop* case as the logical next step after the *Obergefell* decision. Baude emphasized that the case featured "arguments about how broadly the principles of *Obergefell* reach both in the law and society as a whole. The question is whether *Obergefell* was supposed to end the conversation with a definitive victory for one side, or whether there are still further questions to fight over."[36]

Charlie Craig (left) and David Mullins (right) asked the Masterpiece Cakeshop to create a wedding cake for them. The shop owner refused, saying that he opposed same-sex marriage on religious grounds.

Refusing to Advance a Message

To Phillips, the owner of the cake shop, the case was not about discrimination at all. Instead, it was about free speech and artistic expression. It pained Phillips that editorial writers compared him to Southern segregationists who refused to serve African American customers on bogus religious grounds. Phillips was quick to point out that he never refused service to a customer due to race, creed, color, or sexual orientation. He had no objection to baking cakes for gay people; he only objected to baking a cake specifically for a gay wedding. Because same-sex unions conflict with his Christian beliefs, he feels that designing a cake to celebrate a same-sex marriage would force him to make a statement of which he strongly disapproves. In discussing Craig and Mullins's request, Phillips claimed he offered to provide them with other baked goods that did not feature a message. At that point, he said, the couple stormed out of his shop.

Nonetheless, legal experts question whether Colorado is really forcing Phillips to convey any kind of message. Aziz Huq, a professor of law at the University of Chicago, says, "When a vendor produces a product for a customer we usually don't think she's thereby expressing her own views."[37] The ACLU attorneys representing Craig and Mullins note that Phillips did not have to write anything on a cake that specifically supported gay marriage. And Phillips refused to bake any cake for the couple, not just a custom-made one. That, the attorneys say, is a textbook example of discrimination. Legal analyst Lopez feels there is also a deeply personal angle to consider:

> When someone is denied a service, the harm doesn't come just from the fact that he will now have more trouble getting, say, a wedding cake. The harm is also rooted in the fact that another person is telling someone that he is not worthy of something everyone else is worthy of just because of his sexual orientation, race, or some other aspect of his identity.[38]

Is Designing a Cake a Form of Speech?

Phillips offered two main arguments in his defense. First is that the Free Exercise Clause allows him to express his religious beliefs openly in society. Second is the claim that Colorado is illegally

Masterpiece Cakeshop owner Jack Phillips decorates a cake in his Lakeland, Colorado, bakery.

forcing him to use his art and skill as a baker to convey a message he finds morally unacceptable.

Most legal scholars agreed that Phillips's first argument fell short. The Supreme Court has long held that allowing religious exceptions to general laws, such as those against discrimination, would create a tangle of competing purposes and beliefs. However, legal experts found his second argument more convincing. In past cases, people have been allowed to opt out of speech to which they object. For example, schoolchildren are not required to say the Pledge of Allegiance in class, and drivers may cover up a state motto they disagree with on a license plate.

The key question seemed to be whether the act of designing a cake could be considered a protected form of speech.

A Tainted Process

On June 4, 2018 the Supreme Court ruled 7-2 in favor of Phillips. The court surprised legal observers by focusing on the Colorado Civil Rights Commission, the board that originally heard the case against Phillips. The court went back to records of the commission's public hearings and found them troubling. The commission basically said that regardless of his beliefs, Phillips must either bake cakes for gay weddings or get out of the cake business. The justices stated that the commission demonstrated such open hostility toward Phillips' religious beliefs that it violated his First Amendment rights. As Justice Anthony Kennedy wrote in his lead opinion:

> As the record shows, some of the commissioners at the
> . . . public hearings endorsed the view that religious be-
> liefs cannot legitimately be carried into the public sphere
> or commercial domain, disparaged Phillips' faith as despi-
> cable . . . and compared his invocation of his sincerely held
> religious beliefs to defenses of slavery and the Holocaust.
> No commissioners objected to the comments. . . . The
> comments thus cast doubt on the fairness and impartiality
> of the Commission's [handling] of Phillips' case.[39]

The Supreme Court's narrow ruling left open the question of whether other bakers, photographers, or florists could be cited for discrimination should they decline to provide services for a same-sex wedding. The issue seems destined for the Supreme Court once again in the near future.

The Fear of Silencing Religious Voices

Despite the outcome in *Masterpiece Cakeshop*, supporters of religious liberty fear that, in the wake of *Obergefell*, voices opposed to same-sex marriage are being silenced. They say the idea of tolerance for all viewpoints is being overwhelmed by discrimination claims and hostility to faith-based objections. According to Daniel Payne of the Student Free Press Association,

> It has become devastatingly clear that virtually the entirety of the gay-marriage activist effort was built on a lie. That lie, repeated *ad nauseam* [over and over], was this: gay marriage will affect nobody outside of the gays who wish to partake in it. . . . We did not actually need to nationalize gay marriage to realize [the truth]. We have had examples for years from the states that already legalized the practice. Combined with the growing public hostility towards supporters of traditional marriage, it is impossible at this point to deny that gay marriage is a growing and serious threat to the liberty of those who disagree with it.[40]

Payne believes devout business owners are asking for trouble if they show opposition to same-sex marriage. As an example, he points to Melissa and Aaron Klein, the Christian owners of Sweet Cakes by Melissa in Gresham, Oregon. Much like Jack Phillips, the husband-and-wife bakers declined to make a wedding cake for a same-sex wedding. Claiming emotional and mental suffering from the refusal, the lesbian couple, Rachel and Laurel Bowman-Cryer, took their complaint to the state. Oregon's labor commissioner, Brad Avakian, not only fined the bakers $135,000, but he also forbade them to air their views on same-sex marriage in public. On their Facebook page, the Kleins wrote, "This effectively strips us of all our first amendment rights. According to the state of Oregon we neither have freedom of religion or freedom of speech."[41]

The Kleins soon found that longtime associates among florists and photographers no longer would work with them. After paying the fine, and with their income cut in half, the Kleins were forced to close their shop in 2013. John Stonestreet, host of the Christian radio broadcast *BreakPoint*, thinks the huge fine is Oregon's punishment for the Klein's beliefs. "A fine that high," says Stonestreet, "is the Commissioner telling the Kleins, not only are you wrong, you're evil. You need to be put out of business."[42] The bakers' appeals on grounds of religious liberty and free speech have not been successful.

"A fine that high is the [Oregon labor] Commissioner telling the Kleins, not only are you wrong, you're evil. You need to be put out of business."[42]

—John Stonestreet, the host of the Christian radio broadcast *BreakPoint*

For Some, a Worrisome Trend

Defenders of religious liberty see a worrisome trend of believers having their rights of free exercise and free speech curbed. The owners of Liberty Ridge Farm in Albany, New York, a popular rental spot for public and private events, denied a lesbian couple's phone request to hold their wedding on the property. The call was recorded, a judge reviewed the recording, and the owners were fined $13,000 for discrimination on the basis of sexual orientation. The owners and their staff also had to undergo sensitivity training classes. Another example from Harrisburg, Pennsylvania, made national news. The editor of *PennLive/The Patriot-News* announced the paper would no longer accept or print letters or opinion pieces that expressed opposition to same-sex marriage. Many opponents had argued their position on religious grounds.

Refusing to Provide Services for a Same-Sex Wedding Is Illegal Discrimination

The ACLU believes that photographers, florists, and other businesses have no right to refuse services for same-sex weddings because of religious objections. Joshua Block, a senior staff attorney at the ACLU, says such a refusal is discriminatory.

> No court has ever held that a business has a First Amendment right to discriminate in the commercial marketplace. For over 150 years, states have passed public accommodation laws saying that if a business voluntarily decides to open its doors to the public, they can't pick and choose which customers they will serve. . . .
>
> When you make the decision to hold yourself out as a business that serves the general public, you have to be willing to actually serve the general public, which includes a diverse group of people whose values and beliefs may be different than the values and beliefs of the business owner. Selling commercial wedding photography services, like selling a wedding cake or a flower arrangement, does not mean that a business owner endorses a customer's marriage. Everybody has the right to express their views on whatever subject they wish, and that includes business owners. But every business has to play by the same rules in the public marketplace.

Joshua Block, "Photography Businesses Don't Have a First Amendment Right to Discriminate," ACLU, April 7, 2014. www.aclu.org.

After a spate of protests, the paper clarified its policy. Some discussion of the issue would be allowed as long as it did not descend into hate speech.

The Becket Fund for Religious Liberty notes that taking a stand against gay marriage can be expensive. Across the nation, scores of antidiscrimination lawsuits have been triggered by reactions to gay marriage by religious believers. The Becket Fund neither sup-

Refusing to Provide Services for a Same-Sex Wedding Is Not Illegal Discrimination

Trent Horn is a religious scholar at the Catholic advocacy group Catholic Answers. Horn contends that photographers, florists, and other service providers should be able to refuse to work same-sex weddings as a matter of conscience.

> I think the solution to the dilemma of respecting conscience vs. preventing unjust discrimination has to come down to something like this: No private business should be forced to take part in an activity that makes it appear the business owner supports something he considers morally objectionable.
>
> This way of formulating the principle should take the sting out of the objection that "right to refuse service" laws allow business owners to essentially tell minority groups, "We don't serve your kind here.". . .
>
> If I were a lawyer, I would not help someone win an illicit divorce case, because I believe divorce (in the case of a valid marriage) is immoral, and I want no part in that activity. Likewise, if I were a photographer, I would not participate in a same-sex wedding because I have moral objections to that activity as well. . . .
>
> The bottom line is, no one should be forced to participate in an activity he finds to be morally wrong.

Trent Horn, "Conscience and the Right to Refuse Service," Catholic Answers, March 6, 2014. www.catholic .com.

ports nor opposes same-sex marriage. Yet in a court briefing for a same-sex marriage case, Becket representatives declared, "The scholarly consensus is that the threat to religious liberty is real."[43]

The LGBT (lesbian, gay, bisexual, and transgender) community and its supporters also see a threat—to hard-fought rights for people of different sexual orientations. They view the increased number of antidiscrimination lawsuits as a good thing overall. But

Some same-sex couples seeking wedding-related venues and services have encountered pushback from people who contend that their religious views prevent them from providing those services. Many of these incidents are being challenged in the courts.

some, like William Eskridge Jr., find themselves torn. Eskridge, a professor of constitutional law at Yale Law School, describes himself as openly gay and openly religious. He realizes there are strong arguments on both sides. "Fundamentalist Protestants, Catholics, Orthodox Jews, Muslims, Mormons—it's a big chunk of America," says Eskridge. "Decent people. They feel they are under siege by government. Many have no problem with gay customers. They just don't want to participate in the choreography of gay weddings."[44]

A Clash over Adoption Rights

Same-sex couples and religious opponents also clash over adoption rights. This issue receives less attention than gay marriage, but it can lead to bitter disputes among those involved. The case of Kristy and Dana Dumont is an important test. After eleven years of marriage, the couple began to think about adoption.

They found a child-friendly house in Dimondale, Michigan, with a couple of spare bedrooms and a large fenced-in backyard. The neighborhood was diverse and located in a good school district. Dana got on an e-mail list from Michigan's Department of Health and Human Services seeking families for foster care or adoption. The e-mails convinced the Dumonts to act. As Kristy recalls, "When you click on emails and you can see pictures of the kids and stories of the kids, it starts tugging on your heartstrings."[45]

The couple contacted two state-funded agencies for child placement. They asked about adopting a child through the foster care system. But both Catholic Charities and Bethany Christian Services turned them down, explaining that they do not work with same-sex couples. Left unsaid was that the agencies refused because their religious beliefs led them to reject same-sex marriage. "It was kind of a slap in the face," Dana says. "They didn't even know us. How could you say no to people who you don't even know?"[46] The Dumonts thought about how the agencies were denying children—more than thirteen thousand in the state's welfare system—a chance to live in a stable, loving home. They and another same-sex couple enlisted the ACLU to sue Michigan's Department of Health and Human Services and the Children's Services Agency on their behalf.

> "It was kind of a slap in the face. They didn't even know us. How could you say no to people who you don't even know?"[46]
>
> —Dana Dumont on being unable to adopt a child because she was in a same-sex marriage

Opposition and Opportunities

In the suit, ACLU lawyers argue that the state of Michigan was aware that some of the adoption agencies they hired were rejecting prospective families due to religious bias against same-sex couples. The ACLU claims this is unconstitutional in two ways. It violates the Establishment Clause, which bars use of religious criteria in providing government services like foster care and adoption. It also violates the Equal Protection Clause by discriminating against same-sex couples. As the ACLU notes, Michigan's policy harms the most at-risk children by denying them access to loving families that could provide good care.

Michigan is not the only state with adoption policies hostile to same-sex couples. North Dakota, Virginia, and Mississippi all have laws that specifically allow placement agencies to reject same-sex couples on religious grounds. In 2017 similar laws were passed in Alabama, South Dakota, and Texas. Some states also allow a religious agency to turn down families of a different faith or those headed by a single parent. The Michigan case marks the first time such a law has been challenged in court.

Despite faith-based opposition in these states, the outlook overall shows increasing opportunities for same-sex adoption in America. In 2015, the year same-sex marriage became legal, there were forty-four thousand children being raised by twenty-eight thousand same-sex couples, and those numbers continue to grow. Research shows that same-sex couples are almost three times more likely to adopt than heterosexual couples.

The changes and disruptions brought about by the legalization of gay marriage are still being processed throughout the United States. Justice Anthony Kennedy, who wrote the court's lead opinion in both *Obergefell* and *Masterpiece Cakeshop*, can show concern for the dignity of same-sex couples one moment and then worry about hostility toward religion the next. Like Kennedy, the nation itself will have to work out the proper balance between two starkly different visions of America.

CHAPTER 4

Political Advocacy from the Pulpit

On a day designated the National Day of Prayer, President Trump put on display his administration's support for religious liberty. The executive order Trump signed on May 4, 2017, promised to protect political and religious speech by any individual, house of worship, or religious group. The order directs the Treasury Department not to take "adverse action"[47] against churches for political speech. The main target of the executive order is an old law that bars churches from endorsing or opposing political candidates. Trump's order also defended the freedom of health care workers not to perform certain medical procedures they might object to on religious grounds.

Religious leaders of many faiths attended the signing ceremony in the Rose Garden at the White House. They listened to the president stress what he considered the order's urgent purpose. "For too long the Federal government has used the power of the state as a weapon against people of faith," Trump said, "bullying and even punishing Americans for following their religious beliefs."[48] He encouraged ministers and preachers and rabbis to speak boldly from the pulpit without fear of pushback from the government.

A Wide Range of Reactions

Predictably, the order brought a wide range of reactions. Evangelical Christian leaders like Russell Moore of the Southern Baptist Convention heartily approved of Trump's order.

"The very fact that religious freedom is part of the conversation and religious freedom is being affirmed I think is a step in the right direction,"[49] said Moore. Later he tweeted that much more needed to be done on the issue, mainly in Congress. The Reverend Samuel Rodriguez, president of the National Hispanic Christian Leadership Conference, urged the repeal of laws that interfere with religious liberty and political activity. Rodriguez declared that in America today "sincerely held beliefs are subject to not only social ridicule but also legal retribution [payback]."[50]

Civil rights groups took the opposite tack. Anthony D. Romer, the executive director of the ACLU, promised to fight the order in court. He accused Trump of ignoring the wall of separation and using religion to court conservative voters. "President Trump's efforts to promote religious freedom are thinly-veiled efforts to unleash his conservative religious base into the political arena while also using religion to discriminate," said Romer. "We will see Trump in court, again."[51]

> "My job as a priest is not to endorse a politician of any particular political persuasion."[52]
>
> —Randy Hollerith, the dean of the National Cathedral

Many religious leaders shared the ACLU's concerns about the executive order. Randy Hollerith, the dean of the National Cathedral and one of the leading Catholic voices in the nation, thought the order would only divide the country further. "My job as a priest is not to endorse a politician of any particular political persuasion," said Hollerith. "This move will politicize churches, distract us from our intended mission and further polarize the people we are attempting to unite."[52]

Taking Aim at a Tax Code Amendment

Trump's order took aim at the so-called Johnson Amendment. This change to the US tax code was introduced by then-senator Lyndon B. Johnson. When Congress passed the amendment in 1954, it was not considered controversial. The

President Donald Trump signs an executive order that protects political speech by religious entities and health care workers who refuse to perform medical procedures on religious grounds.

Johnson Amendment is part of a section that creates a trade-off for nonprofit groups like churches, charities, and universities. In order to keep their tax-free status, such groups must not "participate in, or intervene in (including the publishing or distributing of statements), any political campaign on behalf of (or in opposition to) any candidate for public office."[53] In other words, churches and groups claiming tax-free status cannot make statements for or against candidates or collect contributions for political campaigns. Pastors are forbidden to endorse candidates from the pulpit.

Of course, the clergy in churches, synagogues, and mosques have free speech rights just as all Americans do. Nonpartisan church efforts to educate voters are perfectly legal, as are church-sponsored drives to register voters. Churches are free to publish voting guides about current issues. Pastors also may speak their minds on social and political questions.

In practice, the Internal Revenue Service (IRS) almost never enforces the Johnson Amendment against churches or other religious organizations. For example, in 2008, groups such as the Alliance Defending Freedom, a conservative nonprofit group of ministers, began to encourage preachers to defy the law and deliver sermons in favor of their preferred candidates. Yet according to a report in the *Washington Post*, the IRS audited only one of about two thousand of these defiant clergy and did not issue a punishment in that case.

Some churches and religious groups would like to see the Johnson Amendment abolished. They view it as an unconstitutional limit on free speech and religious liberty. At the National Prayer Breakfast in February 2017, Trump promised "to get rid of and totally destroy the Johnson Amendment,"[54] but repealing it requires a vote by Congress. Trump's executive order was intended to hamstring the law. However, as some observers have pointed out, the order actually will have little effect. Although the ban on endorsing candidates from the pulpit remains in place, there is little chance it will be enforced. And even if it were enforced, churches can still make implied (or indirect) endorsements without fear of sanction. The Reverend Timothy McDonald III, the senior pastor at the First Iconium Baptist Church in Atlanta, Georgia, says the idea that Trump's executive order gives him the ability to speak freely is nonsense. As McDonald explains,

> **"Under the Johnson Amendment, I have always been and remain free to speak plainly from the pulpit on the issues."[55]**
>
> —The Reverend Timothy McDonald III, the senior pastor at the First Iconium Baptist Church in Atlanta, Georgia

Under the Johnson Amendment, I have always been and remain free to speak plainly from the pulpit on the issues, to conduct voter registration drives at my church, to get out the vote, to host candidate forums, and even to make endorsements in my role as a private citizen. Those in my faith community know that I am already free to speak about the issues of the day because I do so regularly.[55]

A Question of Money

Regulating political speech among churches is a question of money. The Johnson Amendment exists to keep nonprofit groups such as churches and charities from becoming funnels for campaign cash. Wealthy special interests and individuals would love to take advantage of the special tax status of churches in order to make tax-deductible donations to political campaigns. The money these interests contribute to a church could then be passed on to a candidate to buy political ads or fund the campaign. The Johnson Amendment creates an important barrier between churches and political money. The Reverend McDonald calls the Johnson Amendment "an essential levee that keeps the murky tides of secret money from flooding into our sanctuaries."[56]

Despite President Trump's outburst, there is little support for repealing the law. A majority of Americans oppose letting houses of worship endorse political candidates. According to a 2016 Pew Research Center poll, 71 percent of Americans support the Johnson Amendment. And no religious groups favor its elimination. Among white evangelicals, only 36 percent want churches to be able to support candidates. The percentages are even lower for Catholics (25 percent), mainstream white Protestants (23 percent), and black Protestants (19 percent). Shortly after Trump issued his executive order, more than thirteen hundred faith leaders signed an open letter to the White House that warned against weakening the Johnson Amendment. Legal experts also noted that in *Regan v. Taxation with Representation* (1983), the Supreme Court had ruled that banning political activities by tax-exempt organizations was constitutional. Rash talk about repealing the Johnson Amendment seemed unrealistic.

The Branch Ministries Case

The Johnson Amendment received a legal test in the year 2000. In the last days of the 1992 presidential election, Branch Ministries, an evangelical church group in Vestal, New York, paid for a series

Churches Should Not Be Allowed to Endorse Political Candidates

In 2017 Republicans in Congress introduced a tax bill that would allow churches to campaign for political candidates without sacrificing tax-free status. In an opinion piece for the *Houston Chronicle*, ministers Barkley Thompson, Tommy Williams, and Steve Wells explained their opposition to the bill:

> The so-called "Johnson Amendment" has worked for more than 60 years to ensure that our charitable sector remains nonpartisan, allowing churches and other organizations to focus on their missions to improve the common good. . . .
>
> Our congregations each contain Republicans, Democrats and Independents. We gather together, not because of a political affiliation or ideology, but because of our desire to know and serve God better. Nothing about endorsing a candidate will help any of our communities of faith know or serve God better. . . .
>
> Our federal elected officials should heed the call from more than 4,200 faith leaders, more than 5,500 nonprofit organizations and more than 100 national and state denominational and religious organizations who are asking to keep the "Johnson Amendment" protections in place. No one who cares about the health and vitality of our religious communities wants to see them turned into partisan soapboxes.

Barkley Thompson, Tommy Williams, and Steve Wells, "Why Churches Shouldn't Endorse Political Candidates," *Houston Chronicle*, November 17, 2017. www.houstonchronicle.com.

of full-page ads in major newspapers urging Christians not to vote for Arkansas governor Bill Clinton for president. The ads bore the headline "Christians Beware. Do not put the economy ahead of the Ten Commandments." They attacked Clinton for holding positions on abortion, birth control, and homosexuality that the authors considered sinful. At the time, Branch Ministries enjoyed special tax protection as a church, calling itself the Church at Pierce Creek.

The IRS was alerted to the fine print at the bottom of the ads naming Branch Ministries and declaring "Tax-deductible donations for this advertisement gladly accepted."[57]

As a result, the IRS chose to investigate. Citing the ad's political content, the IRS revoked the ministry's tax-exempt status under the Johnson Amendment in section 501(c)(3) of the tax code—the first and only time it has taken such action. Branch Ministries sued the IRS in federal court, claiming its decision

Churches Should Be Allowed to Endorse Political Candidates

Jay Sekulow, the chief counsel of the American Center for Law and Justice in Washington, DC, believes religious leaders should be able to support political candidates from the pulpit as part of their religious mission.

> Religious leaders are muzzled by the IRS law [the Johnson Amendment]. While they can speak out for themselves in their individual capacity, they are barred from either supporting or opposing a political candidate in their role as head of a tax-exempt organization. . . .
>
> That's absurd. The prohibition makes no sense and has far-reaching implications. It censors pastors in the pulpit. And it turns the IRS, which was originally designed to collect revenue for the general treasury, into the speech police. . . .
>
> The time has come to give religious leaders unbridled free speech. . . . Such a move won't result in churches or religious organizations being turned into political machines. It will make it easier, though, for religious leaders to speak out clearly about the issues and candidates that shape the lives and affect the future of millions of people of faith.

Jay Sekulow, "Should Religious Leaders Be Able to Endorse Political Candidates?," American Center for Law and Justice, 2012. https://aclj.org.

violated the church's right to free exercise of religion under the First Amendment and the RFRA. Attorneys for Branch Ministries complained it had been unfairly singled out for political reasons, noting that many other churches had endorsed candidates from the Democratic Party with no penalty. However, the US District Court and the Court of Appeals for the District of Columbia both upheld the IRS's action. The appeals court noted that although other churches may have engaged in political activity, none took out political ads in national newspapers to spread their views. The court added that if Branch Ministries wanted to enter into electoral politics, it must incorporate as a separate political action committee (PAC) under a different section of the tax code.

A History of Mixing Religion and Politics

Political activity like that in the Branch Ministries case is certainly nothing new. The United States has a long history of religious groups plunging into sharp political fights. Americans of many different churches and faiths consider their beliefs part of a distinct political outlook. "Liberal Christians think their liberalism is a natural expression of their Christian faith," says political writer Barton Swaim, "and conservative Christians think the same of their conservatism."[58] Swaim goes on to note that up until the 1970s, most religious groups that joined their faith to political action did so to pursue liberal goals.

For example, many leading voices that spoke out against slavery and, later, segregation, were religious ones. The most radical antislavery movements of the early nineteenth century were fueled by the so-called Second Great Awakening, a Protestant religious revival. The civil rights crusade of the 1950s and 1960s was led by the Baptist minister and activist Dr. Martin Luther King Jr. Church leaders often have campaigned for equal rights among women, racial minorities, and people of different sexual orientations. During the 1970s, as some churches began to pursue more radical left-wing social and economic goals, right-wing evangelical groups responded with political movements of their own.

Issues of tax-exempt status did not arise in the United States until Congress passed a federal income tax in 1916. By common-law tradition, churches were not taxed. Charities and other non-profit groups also were held exempt from paying taxes. However, in 1934 Margaret Sanger's American Birth Control League, the forerunner of Planned Parenthood, became the first nonprofit organization to have its tax-exempt status revoked for political activity. Sanger's group—which was not faith based—lobbied state legislatures and town councils to legalize abortion and birth control.

Charities and houses of worship were still free to endorse political candidates until passage of the Johnson Amendment in 1954. Senator Johnson pushed through the amendment not to obstruct churches but to foil a political rival. Dudley Dougherty, a

The American Birth Control League, founded by Margaret Sanger (pictured), became the first nonprofit organization to have its tax-exempt status revoked because of political activity. The organization lobbied for legalized abortion and birth control.

Catholic rancher in Texas who was running against Johnson for the US Senate, was counting on large contributions from a tax-exempt nonprofit group called the Committee for Constitutional Government. As a follower of the rabid anticommunist Senator Joseph McCarthy, Dougherty drew little sympathy in the Senate. The Johnson Amendment passed without fanfare and went un-challenged for the next forty years. Ironically, Johnson himself did not object to mixing religion and politics. He sought church en-dorsements and religious alliances repeatedly in his campaigns.

Pushing the Boundaries

Houses of worship continue to push the boundaries with regard to endorsing candidates. Voters see nothing unusual in politicians appearing in church to garner support. As far back as 2000, Vice President Al Gore campaigned for the White House at several tra-ditionally black churches. At New Jerusalem Full Baptist Church in Flint, Michigan, Gore listened to the pastor urge his flock to pray at bedtime, "The Lord is my shepherd, I shall not vote for George Bush." At another church in Detroit, Gore told the assembly, "I need you to lift me up so I can fight for you."[59] Meanwhile, at Our Lady of the Rosary Roman Catholic Church in Milwaukee, Wisconsin, the Reverend Joseph Noonan railed against candidates who were not pro-life. "I'm not telling you who to vote for," he explained to his parishioners. "I'm telling you who you may not vote for."[60]

More recently, in 2016, presidential candidate Hillary Clinton took to the pulpit just two days before the election. At the Mount Airy Church of God in Christ in Philadelphia, Pennsylvania, Clinton stressed that the future of the country was at stake. She urged church members to help those who might have trouble getting to the polls to cast their votes. Her opponent, Donald Trump, cam-paigned at the Great Faith Ministries, a nondenominational church in Detroit, Michigan. Trump noted the importance of the church to the African American community. He then delivered his usual campaign message about dealing with low-paying jobs and high unemployment. Pundits disagreed on how effective these ap-

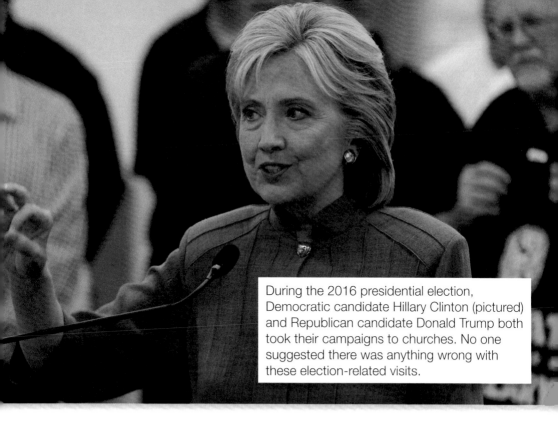

During the 2016 presidential election, Democratic candidate Hillary Clinton (pictured) and Republican candidate Donald Trump both took their campaigns to churches. No one suggested there was anything wrong with these election-related visits.

pearances were, but none suggested there was anything wrong with campaigning inside a house of worship.

Trying to Provoke the IRS

Far from treading softly, some churches are intent on testing the limits of the law. The Alliance Defending Freedom has no worries about triggering an IRS investigation. In fact, the alliance is deliberately trying to provoke the federal agency into ruling against it on the basis of the Johnson Amendment. It believes the law is unconstitutional, violating the religious liberty guarantees of the First Amendment. If cited by the IRS, it intends to challenge the law all the way to the Supreme Court. As Erik Stanley, the senior counsel at the alliance, declares,

> Until 1954, America's pastors had the right to speak freely [if] they exercised that right responsibly. Churches were not turned into political action committees and

party bosses did not set up shop in the basement of churches. Instead, pastors spoke out as they believed their faith intersected with something that was happening in an election. Pastors should have the right to decide that issue for themselves.[61]

Each year, the group sets aside one Sunday in early October to focus its protests. On Pulpit Freedom Sunday, preachers who are eager to engage in electoral politics ratchet up their partisan rhetoric. They aim to go well beyond the boundaries set by the Johnson Amendment. At Hope Christian Church in a Maryland suburb of Washington, DC, Bishop Harry Jackson leads an audience mostly made up of African Americans like himself. After the choir sings a few modern hymns to the chords of an electric piano, Jackson turns to the issues of the day. He does not pull any punches in naming politicians. He attacks those who support abortion and same-sex marriage and endorses those who favor strong ties with Israel. "If it had not been for a free pulpit," he has said, "there would not have been an abolitionist movement. . . . It was a free pulpit in the civil rights movement that called for justice."[62]

Across the country, at Skyline Wesleyan Church in San Diego, California, pastor Jim Garlow also delivers a Sunday sermon that is plainly political. He praises favored politicians by name and rallies support for them at the ballot box. Garlow desperately wants the IRS to notice his partisan words. Like thousands of other church leaders on Pulpit Freedom Sunday, he records his sermon and sends it to the IRS in hopes of prodding them to take action. So far, the IRS has refused to take the bait. But these determined ministers continue to seek a reckoning about the Johnson Amendment and the right of clergy to campaign from the pulpit.

In a time of such deep political divisions, religious leaders will no doubt continue to express their views on current issues. However, judging by polls, most citizens prefer that houses of worship stick to religious themes and leave the campaign messages to politicians.

CHAPTER 5

Religion in the Classroom

For Kaylee Cole, the school day at Lakeside High in northwest Louisiana began like any other. She arrived early, had breakfast with friends, and made it to her classroom on time. Soon the public-address system crackled to life with announcements, birthdays, and news about school events. Finally, the principal's voice prompted students to stand for the Pledge of Allegiance. But on that morning, the first day back after the Christmas holiday, something was missing. There was no group rendition of the Lord's Prayer. Kaylee's mom, a Christian herself, had joined with the ACLU to sue the Webster Parish school district for sponsoring prayer and illegally promoting religion. For Kaylee, an agnostic uncertain about her religious beliefs, the absence of the morning prayer ritual was a huge relief. It had always made her uncomfortable. "For somebody like me, and some of the friends I know . . . it does feel like a church,"[63] Cole admitted.

The Pressure to Participate in Religious Activities

Kaylee says the school would pressure students to engage in religious activities in various ways. One teacher posted a giant message on her wall in colored letters: "Want a Change? Pray." Another teacher posted daily objectives for students, including "Worship God," "Study his word," and "Read the Bible."[64] A science teacher insisted that evolution is a fairy tale and recommended Adam and Eve over the big bang. Visiting speakers on topics like drug abuse or drunk driving often would veer into religious advice. The promotion of the Christian religion was so customary at Webster Parish schools that almost all school events, including assemblies, games, and pep rallies, started with a school-sponsored prayer. As the Coles' suit observes, "Graduation ceremonies are frequently held in houses of worship, and at times they resemble religious rituals that include Bible verses and Christian prayers."[65] Kaylee believes these things are more appropriate for a private or parochial school than a public school.

In response to the Coles' suit, the schools in Webster Parish quietly suspended the faith-related activity. Some students bowed their heads silently in place of a prayer. Some gossiped about Cole and her mother meddling with school routine. There were whispers about the Coles doing the devil's work. Many parents complained about the changes. Yet Kaylee knew she and her mom stood on solid ground with regard to the Constitution. According to Kaylee's mom, Christy, "It's an official systematic program of indoctrinating every child in this parish. They indoctrinated all of their parents. Anybody can pray any time they want, wherever they want. They're just not allowed to have a captive audience to do it. And I really feel like Kaylee [has] been part of that captive audience."[66]

> "Graduation ceremonies are frequently held in houses of worship, and at times they resemble religious rituals that include Bible verses and Christian prayers."[65]
>
> —An excerpt from Kaylee Cole's lawsuit against Lakeside High

The Webster Parish School Board's policy permits school officials to allow students a chance to pray or meditate at the start of the day. The policy adds that no student is required to take part in any religious activities at school or after school. As the ACLU points out in the lawsuit, the First Amendment prohibits public schools from sponsoring prayer or promoting religion in the classroom. "When public schools engage in these unconstitutional activities," the suit declares, "they harm schoolchildren by coercing them into religious practices and subjecting them

Students recite the Pledge of Allegiance. In at least one Louisiana public school district, the pledge was just one of the daily rituals. Prayers and other religious activities were common until they were challenged by one family's lawsuit.

to unwelcome indoctrination and religious messages; they harm parents by usurping their right to control the religious upbringing of their children."[67]

A Landmark Case on School Prayer

Prayer in school strikes many people today as a relic of the past. Yet not so long ago saying a prayer in the classroom was generally accepted. The prohibition on school-sponsored prayer in public schools was first established in a landmark case decided in 1962. The case originated in New York State. At the beginning of each school day, students there would recite the Pledge of Allegiance along with a nondenominational prayer created by the New York State Board of Regents. The prayer went as follows: "Almighty God, we acknowledge our dependence upon Thee, and we beg Thy blessings upon us, our parents, our teachers and our Country."[68] To most students, the prayer was simply part of the morning routine.

However, a group of ten parents in New Hyde Park, New York, claimed the prayer was a violation of the Establishment Clause of the First Amendment. Led by Steven Engel, the group sued school board president William Vitale to have the prayer eliminated. The New York Supreme Court and two appeals courts agreed with Vitale, the defendant, that reciting the prayer was voluntary and so did not violate First Amendment protections. But the Supreme Court took a different view. In *Engel v. Vitale*, the court ruled 6–1 (with two justices absent) in Engel's favor.

In his lead opinion, Justice Hugo Black reached back to the early days of the nation to reject the New York school board's official prayer. "It is a matter of history," Black wrote, "that this very practice of establishing governmentally composed prayers for religious services was one of the reasons which caused many of our early colonists to leave England and seek religious freedom in America."[69] For Black, there was no doubt that the prayer promoted religious belief. Neither the neutral character of the prayer nor the fact that reciting it was voluntary could outweigh the limits of the Establishment Clause.

Many people then and now have mistaken the court's ruling for a blanket ban on prayer in public schools. Immediately after *Engel*, school boards and administrators across the nation overreacted by banning any sort of religious expression by students. Angry citizens at the time accused Justice Black and the Supreme Court of kicking God out of the classroom. In reality, however, students are free to pray in school if they so choose. The violation comes in when schools impose a scheduled prayer or somehow pressure students to participate, even if the activity is supposedly voluntary. It took a while, but over time public school officials have recognized this fact. As Charles C. Haynes of the Religious Freedom Center at the Newseum Institute notes,

State-sponsored prayers in schools are unconstitutional. Students, on the other hand, are fully free to pray in public schools—alone or in groups, as long as they don't disrupt the school or interfere with the rights of others. . . . In fact, there is more student religious expression in public schools today than at any time since the 19th century. Far from being "kicked out," God goes to school today through the First Amendment door.[70]

Narrowing the Rules

In the decades after *Engel*, the Supreme Court further narrowed the rules on prayer in a public-school setting. *Wallace v. Jaffree* (1985) addressed an Alabama statute that attempted to skirt the prohibition on organized prayer. The statute allowed schools to set aside time at the start of the day for silent meditation. No specific religion was mentioned and no specific purpose given for the period of silence. However, state lawmakers changed the statute to cover a period of silence for meditation *or voluntary prayer*. That phrase struck a majority of the Supreme Court as an endorsement of religion. The addition led the court to find the Alabama statute a violation of the Establishment Clause. In a lengthy dissent, Justice William Rehnquist expressed the feelings of many who disapproved of the court's views on school prayer. Rehnquist wrote, "It would come as much of a shock to those who drafted the Bill of Rights as it will to a large number of thoughtful Americans today to learn that the Constitution, as construed by the majority, prohibits the Alabama Legislature from 'endorsing' prayer."[71]

> "In fact, there is more student religious expression in public schools today than at any time since the 19th century. Far from being 'kicked out,' God goes to school today through the First Amendment door."[71]
>
> —Charles C. Haynes of the Religious Freedom Center at the Newseum Institute

Two other high-profile cases brought an end to the custom of having a prayer at the beginning of a school event. In 1992 the Supreme Court ruled that inviting a member of the clergy to deliver brief prayers at the beginning and end of a graduation ceremony violated the First Amendment. In 1995 the court reviewed the Santa Fe Independent School District's policy of allowing a

A student takes a few moments to meditate during class. In some districts students are given time for silent prayer or meditation at the start of the day.

selected student to say a prayer at the stadium prior to football games. This policy also was deemed unconstitutional.

A Controversial Banner

Although students retain the right to personal prayer at school, prayers may not be promoted or displayed. In April 2011 a battle emerged over a prayer banner hanging in a high school auditorium in Cranston, Rhode Island. A gift from the 1963 graduating class, the banner had hung there unchallenged for years. The prayer on it was adopted by the student council in 1959, along with school colors and a new mascot. The banner's message was intended to be inspirational to all students:

Our Heavenly Father,

Grant us each day the desire to do our best,

To grow mentally and morally as well as physically,

To be kind and helpful to our classmates and teachers,

To be honest with ourselves as well as with others,

Help us to be good sports and smile when we lose as well
as when we win,

Teach us the value of true friendship,

Help us always to conduct ourselves so as to bring
credit to Cranston High School West.

Amen.[72]

Sixteen-year-old Jessica Ahlquist, a student at Cranston High, objected to the banner. She claimed it was an endorsement of religion and an affront to her beliefs as an atheist. At a meeting of the Cranston school board, offers to alter the banner to deal with Jessica's concerns went nowhere. Many in the community turned against Jessica and her father. One speaker said, "If people want to be Atheist, it's their choice and they can go to hell if they want."[73] Words in support of the banner brought cries of "Amen!" The board finally voted 4–3 to keep the banner in place. With the help of the ACLU, Jessica and her father sued the school to have it removed.

In its defense in district court, the school claimed the banner was a memento of its founding class and thus had an overriding secular purpose. However, the judge ruled that the banner was obviously a prayer and a Christian one at that. He ruled against the school and ordered removal of the banner.

Ahlquist continued to be attacked in the local newspaper and on radio. When

> "It would come as much of a shock to those who drafted the Bill of Rights as it will to a large number of thoughtful Americans today to learn that the Constitution, as construed by the majority, prohibits the Alabama Legislature from 'endorsing' prayer."[72]
>
> —Justice William Rehnquist in his dissent on *Wallace v. Jaffree*

Prayer Should Be Allowed in Public Schools

The religion-based website Beliefnet notes that recent Gallup polls show that 61 percent of Americans support daily prayer in public schools. The editors at Beliefnet offer several reasons why prayer should not be banned in public schools:

> Students of the same faith, and even of different faiths, can band together in unity. Prayer brings people together, to share in worship. . . .

> Along with the values taught and upheld by the school system, prayer lays a foundation for those principles. Prayer can help guide students to make the right decisions, and better choices throughout the school year. . . .

> Being exposed to other religions, tears down the stereotypes of people that follow a certain faith and the culture tied to it. Prayer in schools can be an opportunity for students, teachers, principals, and other school officials to promote religious tolerance and acceptance. . . .

> Certain religions see prayer as a requirement. For example, in the Islamic faith, Muslims have salat time, or ritualistic prayer performed five times during the day. . . .

> The goal with school prayer is to ensure that all religions are equally represented and respected.

Beliefnet, "7 Reasons We Need Prayer Back in Schools." www.beliefnet.com.

sympathetic friends tried to send her flowers, the local florist refused to fill the order. After receiving death threats, Jessica was given a police escort to and from school. To counter the ugly backlash, the Rhode Island State Council of Churches hosted a gathering to stress tolerance and respect for different views. David M. Brown, the executive director of a statewide Baptist group, told the conference, "Those of us who are following Jesus should be saying to Jessica, 'We respect you. We appreciate your raising these important issues for us. . . . Yes, some of us might vigorously (but gently) disagree with your ideas, but that will never, ever prompt us to stop *loving* you.'"[74]

Teaching About Religion

Another divisive issue is teaching about religion in public schools. It is generally agreed that students should learn about the historical

Prayer Should Not Be Allowed in Public Schools

The Freedom from Religion Foundation is dedicated to preserving the wall of separation between church and state. The foundation explains its view that prayer and religious instruction do not belong in public schools:

> Public schools exist to educate, not to proselytize [promote religion]. Children in public schools are a captive audience. Making prayer an official part of the school day is coercive and invasive. What 5, 8, or 10-year-old could view prayers recited as part of class routine as "voluntary"? Religion is private, and schools are public, so it is appropriate that the two should not mix. To introduce religion in our public schools builds walls between children who may not have been aware of religious differences before. . . .
>
> Our public schools are for *all* children, whether Catholic, Baptist, Quaker, atheist, Buddhist, Jewish, agnostic. The schools are supported by *all* taxpayers, and therefore should be free of religious observances and coercion. . . .
>
> School prayer proponents mistake government *neutrality* toward religion as *hostility*. The record shows that religious beliefs have flourished in this country not in spite of but because of the constitutional separation of church and state.

Freedom from Religion Foundation, "State/Church FAQ: The Case Against School Prayer." https://ffrf.org.

backgrounds of different faiths. However, secularists question whether teachers can be trusted to present lessons about the world's religions in an objective way. The Freedom from Religion Foundation, a national nonprofit devoted to issues of separation of church and state, says it receives frequent complaints from parents and students about teachers who take advantage of comparative religion classes to push their own ideas. With increasing diversity in American classrooms, such a reckless approach becomes a serious problem.

The Supreme Court first weighed in on a similar issue in 1948. A community group called the Champaign Council on Religious Education in Illinois was presenting weekly religious instruction for students in public school classrooms. These classes were approved by the local school board. The council consisted of members from several faiths, including Roman Catholic, Jewish, and Protestant. Almost all the students chose to attend the instructional classes, and they were released from regular classes to do so. Terry McCollum, an elementary school student, had been taught that only his parents could provide religious instruction. When he declined to attend the council's classes, Terry was sent to a distant classroom to complete an assignment on his own. He claimed to have felt ostracized and persecuted.

In *McCollum v. Board of Education*, the Supreme Court ruled that the religious classes were unconstitutional. Justice Black declared that the Champaign system was "beyond question a utilization of the tax-established and tax-supported public school system to aid religious groups and to spread the faith."[75]

A Popular Bible Class

Teaching about religion in public schools still sparks controversy today. A public-school district in West Virginia faces a court challenge for a program called Bible in the Schools. Such a program on school time may be a rarity elsewhere, but in Mercer County it has been a staple of the curriculum for decades. Bible in the Schools consists of weekly classes, thirty minutes for elementary

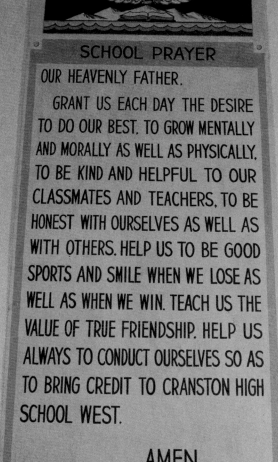

SCHOOL PRAYER

OUR HEAVENLY FATHER.

GRANT US EACH DAY THE DESIRE TO DO OUR BEST. TO GROW MENTALLY AND MORALLY AS WELL AS PHYSICALLY. TO BE KIND AND HELPFUL TO OUR CLASSMATES AND TEACHERS, TO BE HONEST WITH OURSELVES AS WELL AS WITH OTHERS. HELP US TO BE GOOD SPORTS AND SMILE WHEN WE LOSE AS WELL AS WHEN WE WIN. TEACH US THE VALUE OF TRUE FRIENDSHIP. HELP US ALWAYS TO CONDUCT OURSELVES SO AS TO BRING CREDIT TO CRANSTON HIGH SCHOOL WEST.

AMEN

Cranston High School student Jessica Ahlquist objected to a prayer banner (pictured) that hung on the wall of the school auditorium. She contended it was an illegal endorsement of religion and an affront to her atheist beliefs.

school students and forty-five minutes for those in middle school. The school district is quick to point out that attendance is not required, but almost every student takes part. The program garners widespread praise among both parents and students in the district. In fact, community members in Mercer County have raised nearly $500,000 a year to support the program. Nonetheless, in 2017 two new county residents with children of school age sued the district, claiming the Bible in the Schools program is a violation of the Establishment Clause. The plaintiffs were joined by the Freedom from Religion Foundation.

The suit claimed such programs had been banned from public schools dating back to the 1948 *McCollum* ruling. It noted that the program presented biblical material like Sunday school lessons. Bible stories were approached as historical truth. One elementary school lesson read, "If all of the Israelites had chosen to follow the Ten Commandments, think of how safe and happy they would have been."[76]

Before the district court judge could rule on the main issue, the Mercer County school district suspended the Bible in the Schools program indefinitely. Most parents hope the program can be revived. "I think it's a great program mainly because it's the only chance for some of these kids to even see the Bible," said Brett Tolliver, a Mercer County resident. "More importantly, I don't know who it harms. The kids aren't forced to be there."[77] The plaintiffs disagree, saying there were subtle pressures to attend. One plaintiff's daughter was teased for reading a Harry Potter book and told she should be reading the Bible instead. Following the judge's dismissal, both sides claimed victory. But the issue of studying the Bible in public schools seems sure to return.

Challenges in a Changing Society

As the religious and cultural makeup of the United States changes, American public schools will face new challenges regarding school prayer and teaching classes about religion. It will take wisdom and sensitivity to avoid possible pitfalls, with the US Constitution as the best guide.

Introduction: Deep Divisions on Religious Freedom

1. Quoted in Sarah Pulliam Bailey, "HHS Is Targeting Health Workers' Religious Objections. Here's Why," *Washington Post*, January 19, 2018. www.washingtonpost.com.
2. Quoted in Bailey, "HHS Is Targeting Health Workers' Religious Objections."
3. Quoted in National Constitution Center, "Amendment I: Freedom of Religion, Speech, Press, Assembly, and Petition." https://constitutioncenter.org.
4. Nigel Barber, "Why Religion Rules American Politics," *Huffington Post*, July 20, 2012. www.huffingtonpost.com.
5. Quoted in Tom Gjelten, "In Religious Freedom Debate, 2 American Values Clash," NPR, February 28, 2017. www.npr.org.

Chapter 1: The Wall of Separation

6. Quoted in *Wall Street Journal*, "Democrats and 'Dogma,'" September 7, 2017. www.wsj.com.
7. Quoted in *Wall Street Journal*, "Democrats and 'Dogma.'"
8. Cathleen Kaveny, "No, Dianne Feinstein Is Not an Anti-Catholic Bigot," *Washington Post*, September 21, 2017. www.washingtonpost.com.
9. Quoted in USConstitution.net, "Jefferson's Wall of Separation Letter." www.usconstitution.net.
10. Quoted in Merrill D. Peterson, "Jefferson and Religious Freedom," *Atlantic*, December 1994. www.theatlantic.com.
11. Quoted in Legal Information Institute, "Everson v. Board of Education of the Township of Ewing," Cornell Law School. www.law.cornell.edu.

12. Erwin Chemerinsky, "Why Church and State Should Be Separate," *William & Mary Law Review*, vol. 49, no. 6, 2008. http://scholarship.law.wm.edu.
13. Quoted in Legal Information Institute, "Everson v. Board of Education of the Township of Ewing."
14. "Proclamation Appointing a Day of Thanksgiving and Prayer, 11 November 1779," Founders Online. https://founders.archives.gov.
15. Daniel Dreisbach, "The Mythical 'Wall of Separation': How a Misused Metaphor Changed Church-State Law, Policy, and Discourse," Heritage Foundation, June 23, 2006. www.heritage.org.
16. Quoted in Bill Mears, "Supreme Court Weighs Ten Commandments Cases," CNN, March 7, 2005. www.cnn.com.
17. Mark David Hall, "Religious Accommodations and the Common Good," Heritage Foundation, October 26, 2015. www.heritage.org.
18. Quoted in David Davenport, "Congress Actually Decided the Hobby Lobby Case Decades Ago," *Forbes*, June 30, 2014. www.forbes.com.
19. Quoted in Erin McClam, "Religious Freedom Restoration Act: What You Need to Know," NBC News, March 30, 2015. www.nbcnews.com.
20. Catherine Rampell, "Americans Are Entitled to Religious Freedom, but There Are Limits," *Washington Post*, July 2, 2015. www.washingtonpost.com.

Chapter 2: Protecting Women's Health

21. Quoted in *Guardian*, "Obamacare Faces Religious Challenge in Supreme Court," March 23, 2014. www.theguardian.com.
22. US Supreme Court, "Opinions of the Court—2013: Burwell v. Hobby Lobby." www.supremecourt.gov.
23. US Supreme Court, "Opinions of the Court—2013."
24. Quoted in Richard Wolf, "Justices Rule for Hobby Lobby on Contraception Mandate," *USA Today*, June 30, 2014. www.usatoday.com.
25. Quoted in Emily Arrowood and Thomas Bishop, "Conservative Media Celebrate Hobby Lobby Decision by Mocking Women's Access to Contraception," Media Matters for America, June 30, 2014. www.mediamatters.org.

26. Quoted in Wolf, "Justices Rule for Hobby Lobby on Contraception Mandate."
27. Quoted in Michelle Goldberg, "Alito's 'Hobby Lobby' Opinion Is Dangerous and Discriminatory," *Nation*, June 30, 2014. www.thenation.com.
28. US Supreme Court, "Opinions of the Court—2013."
29. Micah Schwartzman, Richard Schragger, and Nelson Tebbe, "The New Law of Religion," *Slate*, July 3, 2014. www.slate.com.
30. Emma Green, "Even Nuns Aren't Exempt from Obamacare's Birth-Control Mandate," *Atlantic*, July 14, 2015. www.theatlantic.com.
31. Quoted in Green, "Even Nuns Aren't Exempt from Obamacare's Birth-Control Mandate."
32. Stephanie Mencimer, "Sometimes Nuns Need Contraceptives, Too," *Mother Jones*, March 22, 2016. www.motherjones.com.
33. Quoted in Pete Williams, "Supreme Court to Hear Religious Objection to Calif. Abortion Law," NBC News, November 13, 2017. www.nbcnews.com.
34. Erwin Chemerinsky, "Clinics Don't Have a Right to Lie About Abortion. This Is an Easy Call Supreme Court," *Sacramento Bee*, February 27, 2018. www.sacbee.com.

Chapter 3: Same-Sex Marriage and Religious Objections

35. German Lopez, "Justice Kennedy Ruled for Same-Sex Marriage. But He Might Flip in a Big New LGBTQ Rights Case," *Vox*, December 5, 2017. www.vox.com.
36. Quoted in Ariane de Vogue, "Supreme Court Set to Take Up LGBT Rights and Religious Liberty," CNN, September 5, 2017. www.cnn.com.
37. Aziz Huq, "Commentary: Here's Why the Supreme Court Wedding Cake Case Is So Complicated," *Fortune*, December 4, 2017. www.fortune.com.
38. Lopez, "Justice Kennedy Ruled for Same-Sex Marriage."
39. US Supreme Court, "Opinions of the Court—2017."

40. Daniel Payne, "The Big Gay Marriage Lie," *Federalist*, July 24, 2015. www.thefederalist.com.

41. Quoted in Zack Ford, "The Newest Argument for Wedding Cake Discrimination," *Think Progress*, July 10, 2015. www.thinkprogress.org.

42. John Stonestreet and Roberto Rivera, "BreakPoint: Sweet Cakes by Melissa, Religious Freedom, Lose on Appeal: Art in the Eye of the Beholder?," *BreakPoint*, January 12, 2018. www.breakpoint.org.

43. Quoted in Alliance Defending Freedom, "Brief Amicus Curiae of the Becket Fund for Religious Liberty in Support of Hollingsworth and the Bipartisan Legal Advisory Group Addressing the Merits." www.adfmedia.org.

44. Quoted in Roger Parloff, "Christian Bakers, Gay Weddings, and a Question for the Supreme Court," *New Yorker*, March 6, 2017. www.newyorker.com.

45. Quoted in Isabel Dobrin, "ACLU Sues Michigan After Same-Sex Couples Seeking to Adopt Are Rejected," NPR, September 23, 2017. www.npr.org.

46. Quoted in Dobrin, "ACLU Sues Michigan After Same-Sex Couples Seeking to Adopt Are Rejected."

Chapter 4: Political Advocacy from the Pulpit

47. White House, "Presidential Executive Order Promoting Free Speech and Religious Liberty," May 4, 2017. www.whitehouse.gov.

48. Quoted in Emily Tillett, "Trump Signs 'Religious Liberty' Executive Order," CBS News, May 4, 2017. www.cbsnews.com.

49. Quoted in Kevin Liptak, "Trump Signs Executive Order to 'Vigorously Promote Religious Liberty,'" CNN, May 4, 2017. www.cnn.com.

50. Quoted in Chelsen Vicari, "Church Leaders React to Trump's Religious Liberty Executive Order," *Juicy Ecumenism* (blog), Institute of Religion and Democracy, May 4, 2017. https://juicyecumenism.com.

51. Quoted in Tillett, "Trump Signs 'Religious Liberty' Executive Order."

52. Quoted in Vicari, "Church Leaders React to Trump's Religious Liberty Executive Order."

53. Quoted in Internal Revenue Service, "Charities, Churches and Politics." www.irs.gov.

54. Quoted in Julie Zauzmer and Sarah Pulliam Bailey, "Trump Wants to End the Johnson Amendment Today. Here's What You Need to Know," *Washington Post*, May 4, 2017. www.washingtonpost.com.

55. Timothy McDonald III, "Destroying the Johnson Amendment Helps Special Interests, Not Churches," *Huffington Post*, September 7, 2017. www.huffingtonpost.com.

56. McDonald, "Destroying the Johnson Amendment Helps Special Interests, Not Churches."

57. Quoted in Grant Williams, "Appeals Court Says IRS Was Right to Strip Church's Tax Exemption," *Chronicle of Philanthropy*, May 1, 2000. www.philanthropy.com.

58. Barton Swaim, "In the Beginning Was the Word," *Wall Street Journal*, March 31, 2018. www.wsj.com.

59. Quoted in Patrick L. O'Daniel, "More Honored in the Breach: A Historical Perspective of the Permeable IRS Prohibition on Campaigning by Churches," Boston College. www.bc.edu.

60. Quoted in O'Daniel, "More Honored in the Breach."

61. Quoted in Eugene Scott, "Pastors Take to Pulpit to Protest IRS Limits on Political Endorsements," CNN, October 1, 2016. www.cnn.com.

62. Quoted in David Shipler, "The Faustian Bargain Between Church and State," *Atlantic*, May 7, 2015. www.theatlantic.com.

Chapter 5: Religion in the Classroom

63. Quoted in Mallory Simon, "What Happened When a Public School Student Sued over Prayer," CNN, January 28, 2018. www.cnn.com.

64. Quoted in Simon, "What Happened When a Public School Student Sued over Prayer."

65. Quoted in Greg Norman, "Louisiana Mom, ACLU Claim School District Promoted Christianity," Fox News, December 19, 2017. www.foxnews.com.

66. Quoted in Simon, "What Happened When a Public School Student Sued over Prayer."
67. Quoted in Norman, "Louisiana Mom, ACLU Claim School District Promoted Christianity."
68. Quoted in Jeffrey Ohene Darko, "Engle v. Vitale," *American Experience*, PBS. www.pbs.org.
69. Quoted in Darko, "Engle v. Vitale."
70. Charles C. Haynes, "50 Years Later, How School-Prayer Ruling Changed America," Newseum Institute, July 29, 2012. www.newseuminstitute.org.
71. Quoted in Belcher Foundation, "Rehnquist's Dissent in Wallace v. Jaffree (1985)." www.belcherfoundation.org.
72. Quoted in Thomas A. Lewis, "A Resident Hears Dissent in Roger Williams' State," Religion & Politics, July 19, 2012. www.religionandpolitics.org.
73. Quoted in Lewis, "A Resident Hears Dissent in Roger Williams' State."
74. Quoted in Lewis, "A Resident Hears Dissent in Roger Williams' State."
75. Quoted in Morgan Chilson, "Prayer in School: 6 Cases Supreme Court Has Ruled On," Newsmax, October 28, 2014. www.newsmax.com.
76. Quoted in Joe Heim, "Judge Dismisses Lawsuit Against W.Va. Public School District That Taught Bible," *Washington Post*, November 19, 2017. www.washingtonpost.com.
77. Quoted in Joe Heim, "West Virginia Public School's Bible Class Heads to Court," *Washington Post*, April 23, 2017. www.washingtonpost.com.

Alliance Defending Freedom

15100 N. Ninetieth St.

Scottsdale, AZ 85260

www.adflegal.org

The Alliance Defending Freedom seeks to unite religious leaders, attorneys, and other advocates in the battle for religious freedom in America. It raises money from donors to fund legal cases involving religious liberty. The group focuses on topics such as religious freedom, pro-life policies, and marriage and family issues.

American Civil Liberties Union (ACLU)

125 Broad St., Eighteenth Floor

New York, NY 10004

www.aclu.org

The ACLU is the nation's leading civil liberties advocate in courts all across America. Its website features analyses of issues relating to religious freedom, such as government promotion of religion, religion and public schools, and the prevention of discrimination based on religion—among other civil liberties topics.

Americans United for Separation of Church and State

1310 L Street NW, Suite 200

Washington, DC 20005

www.au.org

Americans United for Separation of Church and State opposes government aid to private religious schools and supports the wall of separation between church and state. Its website outlines important issues related to religious freedom, such as LGBTQ rights, reproductive rights, discrimination in the name of religion, and political advocacy in houses of worship.

Family Research Council

801 G Street NW
Washington, DC 20001
www.frc.org

The Family Research Council is a Christian-based public policy group that defends religious liberty, the rights of the unborn, and family values. The organization's website contains in-depth analyses of issues related to religious liberty and a blog that covers current news stories about religion and the family.

Books

John Corvino, Ryan T. Anderson, and Sherif Girgis, *Debating Religious Liberty and Discrimination*. New York: Oxford, 2017.

James Fraser, *Between Church and State: Religion and Public Education in a Multicultural America*. Baltimore: Johns Hopkins University Press, 2016.

Frank Lambert, *Separation of Church and State: Founding Principle of Religious Liberty*. Macon, GA: Mercer University Press, 2014.

James Tonkowich, *The Liberty Threat: The Attack on Religious Freedom in America Today*. Charlotte, NC: Saint Benedict, 2014.

Internet Sources

Ryan T. Anderson, "The Continuing Threat to Religious Liberty," *National Review*, August 3, 2017. www.nationalreview.com/2017/08/religious-liberty-under-attack.

Garrett Epps, "Women's Health Takes a Backseat to Religion Again," *Atlantic*, March 23, 2016. www.theatlantic.com/politics/archive/2016/03/womens-health-takes-a-backseat-to-religion-again/475143.

Michelle Goldberg, "Alito's 'Hobby Lobby' Opinion Is Dangerous and Discriminatory," *Nation*, June 30, 2014. www.thenation.com/article/alitos-hobby-lobby-opinion-dangerous-and-discriminatory.

Roger Parloff, "Christian Bakers, Gay Weddings, and a Question for the Supreme Court," *New Yorker*, March 6, 2017. www.newyorker.com/news/news-desk/christian-bakers-gay-weddings-and-a-question-for-the-supreme-court.

Mallory Simon, "What Happened When a Public School Student Sued over Prayer," CNN, January 28, 2018. www.cnn.com/2018/01/23/us/louisiana-school-prayer-lawsuit/index.html.

INDEX

Note: Boldface page numbers indicate illustrations.

abortion, 30–32, 53
adoption, by same-sex couples, 42–44
Affordable Care Act (ACA, 2010), 21
Ahlquist, Jessica, 63–65
Alito, Samuel, 22–24, 25, 28
Alliance Defending Freedom, 48, 55, 75
American Civil Liberties Union (ACLU), 15–16, 37, 40, 43–44, 58–59, 63, 75
Americans United for Separation of Church and State, 16, 75
Avakian, Brad, 38–39

Barber, Nigel, 7
Barrett, Amy, 8, 9
Baude, William, 34
Becerra, Xavier, 31
Becket Fund for Religious Liberty, 40–41
Beliefnet (website), 64
birth control coverage
    under Affordable Care Act, 21
    companies should have to provide, 29
    companies should not have to provide, 28
    percentage of employers offering, 22
Black, Hugo, 12, 14, 60, 66
Block, Joshua, 40
Bowman-Cryer, Laurel, 38
Bowman-Cryer, Rachel, 38
Branch Ministries, 49–52
Brown, David M., 64–65
Burwell v. Hobby Lobby (2014), 21, 22–23, 28, 29

implications of, 24–26

Carolyn, Constance, 27
Champaign Council on Religious Education (IL), 66
Chemerinsky, Erwin, 13–14, 32
churches
    ban on endorsement of political candidates by, 46–47
    should be allowed to endorse political candidates, 51
    should not be allowed to endorse political candidates, 50
    tax-exempt status of, 53
Citizens United v. Federal Election Commission (2010), 26
Clinton, Bill, 18, 50
Clinton, Hillary, 54, **55**
Cole, Kaylee, 57–58
Committee for Constitutional Government, 54
Constitution, US
    religious test for office prohibited by, 9
    See also First Amendment; Fourteenth Amendment
Craig, Charlie, 33, 34, **35**
crisis pregnancy centers, 30–32

Decker, Larry T., 4
Department of Health and Human Services, US (HHS), 4
Division of Conscience and Religious Freedom (Department of Health and Human Services), 4
Dougherty, Dudley, 53–54
Dreisbach, Daniel, 15
Due Process Clause, 34
Dumont, Dana, 42–43
Dumont, Kristy, 42–43
Durbin, Dick, 8